THE SLEUTH
INVESTOR

THE SLEUTH INVESTOR

UNCOVER THE BEST STOCKS
BEFORE THEY MAKE THEIR MOVE

AVNER MANDELMAN

McGraw-Hill

New York   Chicago   San Francisco   Lisbon
London   Madrid   Mexico City   Milan   New Delhi
San Juan   Seoul   Singapore   Sydney   Toronto

1 2 3 4 5 6 7 8 9 0   DOC/DOC   0 9 8 7

ISBN-13: 978-0-07-148185-4
ISBN-10: 0-07-148185-0

This publication is designed to provide accurate and authoritative information in regard to the subject matter covered. It is sold with the understanding that the publisher is not engaged in rendering legal, accounting, or other professional service. If legal advice or other expert assistance is required, the services of a competent professional person should be sought.

—*From a Declaration of Principles Jointly Adopted by*
a Committee of the American Bar Association and
a Committee of Publishers and Associations

McGraw-Hill books are available at special discounts to use as premiums and sales promotions, or for use in corporate training programs. For more information, please write to the Director of Special Sales, Professional Publishing, McGraw-Hill, Two Penn Plaza, New York, NY 10121-2298. Or contact your local bookstore.

This book is printed on acid-free paper.

To Joe Garber, in memoriam, for lessons learned.

ACKNOWLEDGMENTS

To my agent, Victoria Pryor, without whom this book would not have been written; my editor, Jeanne Glasser, without whom this book would not have been published; Professor Ben Friedlander, of the University of California in Santa Cruz, math maven extraordinaire, who set me straight on several issues mathematical; Brian Piccioni, tech analyst numero uno, who set me straight in certain matters technological; Debbie Gray, the marketing prodigy who pointed out where the book was too pointed and where too little; my two smart boys, Ron and Dan, who forbore my writing; Mark, my partner in Giraffe; and most of all, to the clients of Giraffe Capital, for their trust and support.

CONTENTS

AUTHOR'S NOTE

What is legal in one place may not be in another—whether state, province, or country—so please consult a competent local lawyer before attempting any of the methods noted in this book. The cases and examples featured in this book are provided for illustrative purposes only and do not represent real events or real people. Do not invest based on what you read in this book before consulting an investment advisor and a tax advisor. Even if you initially make consistent profits based on what you learn in this book, do not let it go to your head, because you might then put too much into the next investment and that one may fail. Be diligent. Be prudent. Be good. Give to charity. Tell your friends about this book. Visit my Web site at www.thesleuthinvestor.com, and e-mail me about your own sleuthing tips and successes, at am@thesleuthinvestor.com, and I may include them in the next book.

THE SLEUTH INVESTOR

INTRODUCTION: FOOLISH MONEY RIPE FOR THE TAKING

To make money in the stock market, it's not enough to rely on public information. You have to act like a sleuth. You must probe behind the printed surface of SEC files, annual reports, and press releases, and sleuth for those concrete facts that reveal the truth about a company's real value—and its future.

In investment sleuthing you use detection and investigatory techniques to get exclusive, *physical* information about companies in which you are considering investing. Little-known facts about a company can give you a decisive edge when buying or selling that company's stock. With investment sleuthing, you can find out in advance if a company is about to report high growth, learn of a coming disaster that you can short profitably, or anticipate certain mergers and acquisitions right before they occur, and much, much more.

The method is not hard to learn, but it does require a different mind-set; several successful investors, including Philip Fisher and Peter Lynch, have been sleuthing intuitively for years. I, too, have been using this method for a long while, as have several of my professional friends and colleagues. It has helped us accumulate tidy profits away from the public eye, and it also helped me run one of the few tech funds in North America that made money through the bubble years while others lost.

First and foremost, sleuth investing requires that you stop thinking of stocks as mere numbers, documents, legal filings, printed matter, data, or graphs on a screen. Once you finish this book, you will view companies as *physical* entities, and no longer see stock investing as an office-based, bookish activity but rather as an *investigatory field craft*. You will learn to follow the physical movement of products, either directly or indirectly (or pay others to do this for you), and watch for physical signs that forecast financial results almost unerringly. You will learn how to get exclusive information from low-level employees; how to gather such information from a company's clients, suppliers, and other peripherals; and how to glean from a company's surroundings the telltale physical clues for what's coming—legally and ethically. Such clues are there to be seen by those who shut off their Internet screen, leave their office, and go out into the real world to mix with actual people with the aim of getting exclusive information.

You will learn in this book how to do this type of investigation and more. It is my conviction that sleuthing will forever change the way you invest—and the way you look at money and moneymaking. It will also make you richer, perhaps much richer. Just how much is up to you.

WHY I'M SHARING THIS SECRET

Normally, those who have a moneymaking method that works do not want to divulge it, because if others use it, profit for the original users would be reduced. In this case, the amount of foolish money available to be taken by stock sleuths is enormous. There's so much foolish money in the market—money invested unwisely, based on no specific knowledge of the human element, and with no real understanding of what makes one business succeed and another fail—that there is more than enough to go around.

I tried to make this book easy to read and follow, even when it touches on technical topics and investigatory techniques, by organizing the book using the three natural sources for exclusive information: people, product, and plant and periphery. I then included examples culled from my own experience and from that of my investment-sleuthing friends to illustrate important aspects of the method. (The examples use fictitious companies.) The main techniques are set out explicitly, yet if you have a bit of imagination, I am sure that what you read here will trigger your own ideas. Once you start, I'm sure your own sleuthing tricks will, in time, probably differ from mine. Stock sleuthing is subjective; the goal for different practitioners can be the same, but the individual application and methods are as distinctive as those who practice them.

However, one thing is certain: by following this method, you won't be able to avoid making money; and, perhaps equally important, you'll stop losing it to people like me.

HOW I SLEUTHED FOR THE FIRST TIME

Like so many other things in life, my sleuthing developed by accident. I began my career as an engineer, but had always wanted to make money in the market. So after working for a few years, I applied and was accepted to the MBA program at Stanford University's Graduate School of Business. But the available investment and finance courses were less fun than I had imagined. All except one were taught by mathematicians, economists, and accountants, who saw reality only through the prism of numbers, text, and charts. Only one course was different. Professor Steven Brandt taught me how to read anonymous financial statements in order to determine the kind of business the company was in and the kind of problems it likely faced. He also taught me some basic business principles that serve me to this day. Yet, it seemed from my courses that stock investing was all about massaging public data more cleverly than others, and the concepts behind investment disciplines were nearly all mathematical, scientific, financial, and statistical. Even classical methods of picking cheap stocks, like those of Warren Buffett and Ben Graham, were barely mentioned; of foolish money, there was no mention at all.

IF ALL INVESTORS ARE RATIONAL, WHY DO SO MANY LOSE?

I first got an inkling of the existence of foolish money when I sat in the Stanford auditorium for a finance course taught by Professor Bill Sharpe. Sharpe had devised the capital asset pricing model—a close cousin of the efficient market theory (EMT), which led to the creation of index funds, where hundreds of billions of dollars are invested based on no specific knowledge of stocks. That's the foolish money sleuths aim to take.

Index funds came into being because EMT says that no investor can make more money than others in the market without taking on more risk, since whatever information an investor has is also available to all other investors. All investors are presumed to be rational and therefore all buy the same things, which quickly reach an equilibrium price where no one makes any money. The equilibrium price fluctuates randomly, and thus is impossible to predict, says the EMT.

The inevitable conclusion of this thinking is that the only way to make more money than others in stocks is to take a risk by acting without adequate information. This theory (further elaborated by Robert Merton, Harry Markowitz, and other economists who won Nobel prizes for their parts in it) was proven mathematically and thus was accepted by everyone in business schools all over the world, including Stanford Biz, where students labored over obscure terms such as alpha, beta, volatility, and the efficient frontier. Only years later did I hear that Warren Buffett mocked EMT mercilessly with his famous parable of the monkeys. (I'll tell you more about that in Chapter 1.) At the time I didn't know this, or of Buffett, but felt in my bones that EMT was bunkum, even though it was mathematically proven. I knew math well enough (my first degree is in aerospace engineering—yes, rocket science) to pick my way through EMT's Greek letters, and so it was clear to me that its logic hung on a few assumptions that were utterly and clearly foolish, for the following reasons.

First, *finance professors implicitly assumed that the market will behave tomorrow just as it had yesterday*—or else how could different investors with the same (past) data forecast the same (future) equilibrium prices? Some years later, Professor Mordecai Kurz of the Stanford Economics Department would prove with hard data and impeccable math that this assumption was wrong.

Second, and more egregious, *finance professors automatically equated information with symbols*—that is, the secondhand stuff you get from newspapers (and today, the Internet) or other printed matter, as opposed to the raw facts that these letters and numbers describe. It never crossed any academician's mind that you can seek exclusive *physical* information stealthily for yourself, keep mum about it, then use it to take the money of those who buy and sell based only on what everyone else also knows.

So I sat in Bill Sharpe's class for a few weeks, did all the work, found the math interesting, yet thought it completely irrelevant to stock investments. It was as if I, an engineer, were asked to teach you how to build a bridge, but instead of showing you how to attach beams to each other and crosshatch joists, I brought you a spectral analysis of the light reflected off the bridge's surface, showing that it fluctuated randomly with a statistical distribution thus and so. Sure, it would be true, but it would be entirely irrelevant, because it would be *descriptive*, rather than *prescriptive*.

STOCK PRICES VIBRATE—SO WHAT?

Similarly, the fact that stock prices vibrate randomly as they rise or fall slowly to reach their real value, although true, is utterly irrelevant to moneymaking. This, in essence, was my beef with mathematical finance—it told stories (in math, yes, but stories) *about* investments and stocks, rather than showed me *how* to buy good stocks cheaply off other people. So after two weeks of such descriptive mathematical storytelling, I switched to another course, one given by a lively accountant who taught us how to spot financial shenanigans via accounting footnotes. It was almost as much fun as Steve Brandt's class, but still not what I wanted.

The class that finally put me on the path to market enlightenment was a required course called Business Policy, taught by a suave ex-White House intern. His White House experience led him to give us real-world assignments, one of which was to research two competing tech companies in Silicon Valley and judge which was likelier to win in a certain tech market. I liked that assignment a great deal; it was exactly what I was looking for. Because both companies were publicly traded, the research could help me decide which stock was better, and thus also help me invest better in the future.

SECONDHAND ANALYSIS, AIDED BY FIRSTHAND BEER

The class was divided into teams of five. We met twice weekly for two months in the Biz School's Jackson Library to gather data and massage them; then, for the final meeting, we met in the Dutch Goose, which was then the pub where Stanford students went to drink weak California beer and feel very Zen. By that time our team already had a full comparative analysis of the two companies—their products, market shares, corporate structure, and financial statements, for which we also made detailed forecasts.

It was a beautiful piece of work. However, as we sat in the Goose, I saw another group of Biz Schoolers working on the same project. I was able to peek at what they were doing, and I saw that they had nearly the same ideas as we did: market positioning, financial statements analysis, forecasts—the same thing, even the same presentation order. It dawned on me that both presentations were based on the exact same information that someone else had collected, presented, printed, and stored, and the only things we were adding were brainpower, organization, and logic. It further occurred to me that maybe, in an odd way, Professor Sharpe was right. Was rearranging and massaging the same data enough to give us an edge? It is like expert chefs trying to produce a far better stew than other gourmets while using exactly the same ingredients. Both teams—all teams really—were going to produce good work, perhaps even excellent work. Grades, however, would be given on the famous bell curve—only one or two could get an H (Honors), with the majority getting a P (Passing), and very few a failing grade. To win in this efficient grade market, we had to be not just good, but exceptional. Yet nowhere in the course were we taught how to obtain such an edge.

It was then that I had a wild idea. I didn't tell anyone about it because in my academic-induced idiocy I was concerned that it might be viewed as cheating. My idea was to snoop around the two companies in person to get non-numerical data that the other teams did not have—to collect exclusive ingredients for our stew, if you will.

It may not sound brilliant, but you'd be surprised to learn that in no business school course at the time were students ever taught to sleuth for original physical data when it came to stock investing. To this day, no biz school that I know of teaches stock investment as an investigatory field craft. At any rate, I decided to get us some exclusive input—stew ingredients.

The next day I left before noon and drove about 20 miles south of Stanford to Santa Clara, the headquarters of the first company. I parked in the company's lot, walked into the company's lobby and asked the receptionist something—I no longer recall what—chatted with her briefly, then left and sat at Peet's Coffee across the road and waited for the staff to go to lunch.

Feeling like Philip Marlowe, I knew that the group generally went to a specific fast-food joint, and headed there. I went in and feigned pleasant surprise when I spotted her. We both smiled and chatted a bit as we waited to order, so it was natural for me to join her table. When I told her I was a student at Stanford Biz, she got coy and interested (MBAs are a good catch), and so when I asked her about her work, she opened up and told me whatever I wanted to know.

What I aimed for was general background, what the army calls "fiber intelligence." So I listened attentively as she chatted about the general scuttlebutt of who did what to whom in the company. I was ashamed to see she thought I was trying to pick her up, while in truth I was only fishing for information. Finally I asked for her phone number, to ease my conscience. But did I ever get the information I wanted! And it was so good and conclusive that I really didn't have to check out the other company—but I did so anyway the next day. There I chatted with two of that company's junior salesmen in a Chinese restaurant near their office, saying I knew someone who worked for one of their suppliers. They confirmed what I had learned from my first informant, and that afternoon I went back to our final team meeting.

When I told my teammates of my findings, a fierce debate arose over whether what I had done was ethical and whether we could use the information. Some insisted we could not possibly tell the class what I had found—it would sound so ungentlemanly and unprofessional. Yet no one could deny that the information I had was clearly highly relevant. The dilemma was especially acute because our previous theoretical analysis had concluded that Company A would likely win the market share battle, but my sleuthed information was that Company A's president had just been caught in a very compromising position and was going through a divorce—the proceedings of which would likely be bitter and long. It seemed clear to me that the president would likely not be running the company well, nor would the company personnel recover from the shock any time soon. And since the president was a majority owner in the company, he was unlikely to be replaced. The entire saga was known to everyone in the company, in the shopping plaza nearby, and in the local church. But the budding investment scientists at Stanford Biz were so busy with regression analysis and pie charts and accounting footnotes and betas and alphas that they knew nothing of this.

Luckily for our team, the saga was also detailed in public court documents, which could be seen and quoted by anyone who bothered to look them up. So our group could legitimately claim we had gotten it through research. ("Research," please note, was then, and still is, considered getting information from documents, not from receptionists.) We could therefore use the information because it could be documented, yet nobody in the team except me was willing to.

The argument went round and round. Finally, I snapped that investment was war, and "in war you do what you have to do." Our team leader, an A-10 pilot and a Vietnam veteran, nodded sagely, said this was indeed so, cut the argument short, and that was that. We added the court documents as a secret appendix for the professor's eyes only, and skewed the report to have Company B win, noting in passing that management of Company A had "severe personal issues" that would "likely prevent them from dedicating full time to the business." When pressed to elaborate by the entire class at the auditorium where we presented our conclusion, we said it was of a private nature which we would tell the professor only. The class's curiosity was intense, but none of the team members revealed the information in public. We did so in private to the professor, and I ended up getting an H for the course—one of the only two such given. I later won First Prize in Business Policy (The Mason Smith Award) at the end of the MBA program.

Even so, all participants in the work group looked at me askance from that day on, as if I had done something shady, like a spy (or a soldier) who had done the necessary dirty work to keep the state safe, but whose deed had forever stained him. This hurt me and caused me to doubt the wisdom of my actions, so after graduation I went for coffee with the Business Policy professor and told him of my misgivings. He laughed and told me not to worry, and said they did such things in the White House every day. (You'll notice that I refrain from specifying which White House he had served in.) I thanked him, and the following week returned to Canada, where I found a job as a stock market analyst advising pension funds.

If you are wondering about whether I followed up with the receptionist, the answer is that some things neither gentlemen nor spies divulge.

And now we can go into the method itself.

SO WHAT EXACTLY IS A COMPANY, REALLY?

Warren Buffett recommends that you consider a stock as partial ownership in the company behind it. Such a view helps you ignore fluctuations in the stock price and focus on the company's value. If you know the company's true value, and if you can buy its stock much lower than that, all you have to do is wait until the price rises to value. Focusing on the company is what helped Buffett make billions, and it is also the best starting point for the art of stock sleuthing. To make a lot of money in stocks, you must know much more about the company than others do. So let's start with a simple question: *What is a company?*

A company is not its legal charter, nor its annual report, nor its corporate filings—although all are important sources of data (not information, but data)—nor is it a string of historical prices that can be plotted and regressed. Rather, a company is a group of people doing work in an office or a plant, so that other people (the customers) will send them checks. A company, in short, is a *check-receiving work group*. If the work group does good work, the other people (the customers) will send them lots of checks, and then the stock (which is a piece of the company you can buy) will rise. If the work group does bad work (or work that is not as good or as cheap as that done by other work groups), the customers will send fewer checks, and the stock will fall. By direct logic, then, the best source for learning whether you'll get more for your stock than you paid for it is the company's customers—those who send the checks. Thus, if you want to get information that will help you buy stocks that you'll later sell for a higher price, you must talk to the company's customers. Right?

The above is such a simple concept that it should be a no-brainer. But you'd be surprised to learn how few investors talk to the customers of a company whose stock they buy for tens of thousands, hundreds of thousands, or even millions of hard-earned, hard-saved dollars. Even professional investors and analysts—especially professional investors and analysts—are guilty of this omission. In fact, if you want to embarrass any Wall Street or Bay Street analyst, ask him (we'll assume it's a him): Who are the biggest five customers of your favorite stock—say, XYZ Enterprises?

Please note: We are not looking for the names of the five *companies* who are XYZ's biggest customers. We want the names of the *people* in these companies who decide to send the checks that become XYZ's revenues. We want each person's name, age, phone number, office address, background, job title, spending authority, home address, family status, name of spouse, names of kids. Picture, too, if possible. Why do we want this? We want this information because *90 percent of all business is targeted schmooze.*

If you think I'm overdoing it, think again. If you were promoted to the position of XYZ's VP of Sales, the first thing you'd do is meet your salespeople (and get similar information about them); and then you'd say: Bring me the spreadsheet that shows our sales breakdown. I'd like to see who are the biggest five customers who help us pay the rent and electricity for this joint, and my salary and yours, and who will help us all make a hefty bonus. Then you'd say, I want to hear from each salesperson who the individual buyers inside the clients' companies that he or she covers are— the individual human beings who decide to buy our products and send us checks. I want their names and description, their position in their organization, where they sit, who they meet, how much money you think they make, how much of it is in salary and how much in a bonus, and how our product or service helps them *personally* to either rise in their organization or make a higher bonus or both. Then I want to know how they make the buy decision—in person or as part of a team; if as a team, who are the team members, how often do they meet, and where? Finally I'd like to know if these individuals like golf, fishing, car racing, sailing, basketball, or baseball, so I'd be able to decide on what kind of outings to take them, where I can befriend them and hear from them directly why they buy our products, and what we should be doing to make them buy more.

This, at the very least, is what you'd ask for if you were to become XYZ's sales VP. And again, if you think I am overdoing it, check out the briefing books for jetliner salespeople who are about to try to sell a small fleet of their jets to, say, *Saudia*, the Saudi Arabian Airlines. Their briefing books contain some information that, if published in a newspaper, would be mighty embarrassing. I once saw such a briefing book; it looked as if it had been compiled by the CIA (which perhaps had helped, but this is only a supposition).

At any rate, if XYZ's sales VP needs this information to do his job, you, as a stock sleuth aiming to take the foolish money of those who invest based only on public information and price fluctuations, should be aiming for no less.

Yes, of course I understand you cannot possibly find out all of this information. You don't have an organization or the training, but at least you have an ideal to aim for; and besides, you'll be surprised how much of the above you can learn if you ask around, as you'll soon see once we get into the various techniques of gathering information. You can do much more than you think, once you focus on the right things.

CAN YOU FIGHT A WAR WITH PUBLIC INFO?

Basing investment decisions solely on public information is like sending an army into battle based only on public information gleaned from the newspapers. For those who invest in large mutual funds and index funds that invest only on such information, this is bad news. But for stock sleuths like me and my colleagues—and for you, once you learn the techniques—this is very good news, because it shows conclusively that there really are huge amounts of foolish money out there to be had.

Now an important clarification: Just because a company is human, specific, and physical, not mechanical, general, and conceptual, you cannot ignore annual reports, corporate SEC filings, historical prices, and all the other public data, both financial and otherwise, that everyone else knows about. Just because you cannot expect to make a fortune using public information alone, you sure can lose a fortune if you are ignorant of the public data. But you must remember that after you bone up on these details, you shouldn't act on them before you sleuth for *exclusive* information.

HUMAN CONTACT—THE WINNING EDGE

But, you may ask, what if you can't pick up receptionists? Or chat up salesmen in restaurants? What then? No need to worry. First of all, you don't have to pick up anyone. A female sleuth could have gone into Company A's lobby and asked for directions same as I did, then chatted with the receptionist about the photograph of her two adorable nephews behind the switchboard—anything to establish human contact. Then, after bumping into the receptionist at the fast-food joint, the female sleuth would have been just as effective as I was.

Another important aspect to consider is that you don't have to do all the sleuthing yourself. If chatting with new people is not your cup of tea, it might be to the liking of your sister, aunt, even grandmother—and you may be surprised at their readiness to join in your enterprise as an adventure. Or, if you are a member of an investment club, perhaps the amiable retired teacher who just loves talking to people, or the club member who is also a family doctor in whom everyone naturally confides, would agree to sleuth on the club's behalf. It's unimportant if they have no experience. Few know if they are natural at people-sleuthing until they try.

Smaller money management firms can also be fertile grounds for sleuthing talent. This is especially true when assistants and secretaries are included in the talent pool—they can be particularly effective in chatting up counterparts in target companies, and can often find out information that their bosses can't.

THE THREE PHYSICAL ELEMENTS OF ALL SLEUTHING

Sleuthing is about more than chatting up people. Exclusive information resides in three physical aspects of a company, of which people are only one. The three are (by descending order of importance):

1. PEOPLE (the company's own, its customers, and its suppliers)

2. PRODUCT (both the company's own, including services, and those it consumes as supplies, as well as competing products)

3. PLANT (factories or offices where the work is done) and PERIPHERY (everything else that impinges on the company from the outside, or that the company impinges on, and so leaves physical traces). Because it is often hard to see where Plant ends and Periphery begins, this books deals with both together.

In the chapters that follow, I'll discuss all three elements in detail, showing you investigatory techniques useful for each, and illustrating these methods with examples. We'll begin in Chapter 1 with the most important element of the trio: People—that marvelous check-receiving group whose company's stock you aim to buy cheaply to make a fortune.

THE MYSTERIOUS CASH MAKERS

The company's cash makers are the company's people who do the work for which customers send checks. The work can be physical—like drilling holes in the ground to extract platinum, or cutting and bending steel to make cars, or melting and slicing silicon to make microchips. The work can be mental, writing books and articles, or designing and drawing circuit diagrams, or composing jingles for radio commercials. Or it can even be spiritual—like broadcasting a gospel on TV and asking for donations. These activities are all variations of work for which customers send checks.

Now, before you get upset, I am not suggesting that the motivation for all work is strictly to receive checks. People work for a variety of reasons, and I don't intend to touch on these here. I'll cover this topic briefly when we go into the techniques for extracting information from people.

For now, however, it's enough to know that if the work done is good (or better and/or cheaper than others' work) and the customers are worthy, more checks will come. If the work is bad (or insufficiently good or cheap) or the customers are unworthy, the checks will be fewer. The exclusive information you are after will always be about payments (the checks) received by the company—now, and in the future.

STAY PHYSICAL, YOUNG MAN

In sleuthing you zero in exclusively on the concrete elements noted above: the people inside the company, the people outside the company, the work—designing, bending, digging, writing, broadcasting, sending—and finally the checks. These physical activities and objects can all be seen and measured, and you can sleuth them firsthand. How do you do this?

First, divide the people who have the exclusive information you want into three categories:

1. People who work for the company

2. People who work for the customers

3. People who work for providers of products and services (such as suppliers, but also bankers, lawyers, accountants, even caterers) and for peripherals

"Peripherals" include people who work for competitors, the professor who was the PhD thesis advisor for the company's R&D vice president and who would know if that person is a genius or a mediocre talent, people who have worked with key executives previously and have a good sense of their ability, the secretary of the town chamber of commerce who would know if the company has applied for a sewage permit because it intends to expand, or a local real estate agent who would be aware of rumors of a company's property being put up for sale because of a dearth of orders. In this chapter, I present an overview of the people element and cover in detail how to sleuth individuals inside the company. In Chapters 2 and 3 I will tackle customers and suppliers.

SO WHAT IF YOU ARE NOT A DETECTIVE?

In sleuthing there are several obvious difficulties: finding out who the relevant people are, how many you should investigate, and where to look for such information. How can you possibly do all this digging for each of the stocks that you own? After all, you are not a trained detective. And even if you were, this is still a huge task.

The last difficulty can be resolved most readily by a careful selection of the target company, well before you embark on such a great effort and expenditure of time. As Warren Buffett has often advised: It's better to own only a few stocks about which you know a lot, than to own a hundred stocks about which you know very little. I'll leave the solution to the problem of which companies to target for Chapter 7, which discusses this subject. For the purposes of this chapter and the next several ones, I'll assume that the company you want to sleuth is worthy of close and intense scrutiny.

To begin, make a list of the company's most important people and a list of as many people as you can identify who are lower in rank but still important to the company.

PUBLIC SOURCES: WHAT EVERYONE KNOWS

You can learn which people in a company are important via public information—the annual report and various filings, such as the 10K, 10Q, and annual information circulars. You can get all these from the SEC Edgar website (see Appendix A for details), from the company's own website, or by calling or writing the company. The list of important people includes not just the most senior executives and the board of directors (whose pictures often appear in the annual report). It also includes the best salespeople for the top products, the engineers who work on the new versions of the most important products (those products that generate the highest revenues or those for which the company has the highest hopes for growth), and any other internal workers connected to areas or tasks that *you deem* to be most important for the company.

GIVE YOURSELF YOUR MARCHING ORDERS

D eem how? Well, you do have to exercise judgment in determining what the most urgent tasks for the company are at present, as well as the most important questions tied to them. Write all this down. You would, in effect, be acting both as an army general giving a list of "information objectives" to his intelligence chief, and the intelligence chief who is in charge of getting this information. Every army in the world goes through this process periodically, handing its intelligence services lists of regularly updated objectives. Intelligence services usually find answers to only 50 or 60 percent of the key questions, but at least they are sleuthing in the right direction. You will be, too, if you select the right tasks and commit to them in writing. Don't worry if the tasks seem next to impossible to accomplish. If you believe they are key, write them down.

And what if the tasks you figured to be critical do not turn out to be the right ones? Don't worry about that for now. Even if the tasks you choose are not the key ones, the effort to sleuth out exclusive information in any reasonably important area is bound to have two useful effects. First, it will teach you how to sleuth. Second, because your efforts will teach you much more about the company than you could ever hope to learn from public data, the key questions, which at first may have evaded you, will very soon become clear. Trust me on this—I have gone through this process many times, and the convergence of side-digging to mining essentials is rapid. Physical sleuthing has a way of setting you onto the path of the truth very quickly.

But we are jumping too far ahead here. For the moment, assume only that you have prepared a list of the most important positions in the company and that you have names to go with the titles for about half of those positions. Moreover, some of those titles may consist solely of a description, such as "key salesperson for Product X in North America," or "point-person in negotiating debt-rescheduling with the banks." (Knowing that the bank is the Bank of Chicago is better—and even better is the description "Bank of Chicago, 134 First Avenue branch, 1st floor mezzanine.") You also have a list of the key tasks that these important people have to perform successfully if their company is to receive more checks.

The next task is getting to know these people personally as a first step toward your goal of *penetrating* the company.

BEYOND PUBLIC INFORMATION

enetration is an intelligence-services term which I am using here with great caution, because if you do it rashly in commercial life, it can land you in trouble. In the intelligence world, penetration means planting a mole inside the opposition's camp—such as Aldrich Ames in the CIA or Kim Philby in British intelligence. Both men sold their nations' secrets to the Soviets, the first for personal gain (and probably out of petty spite), the second because of misguided ideology. Both betrayed trust. If you try to gather exclusive information in the commercial world via moles like these, both you and the moles will end up in jail, and deservedly so. This is certainly not the kind of "penetration" that I am talking about. What you should aim for is establishing good personal relations with personnel both high and low in the organization that will enable you to chat with them often, as well as visit the company occasionally and be allowed to tour the plant and offices. Hence, you will have opportunities to gather *physical* information with your eyes, ears, and any other sense you can use.

Philip Fisher, author of *Common Stocks and Uncommon Profits* (see Appendix A) and one of the earliest stock sleuths, used to call this "gathering scuttlebutt." He did this for many years by cultivating relationships in Silicon Valley with engineers and company executives with whom he chatted informally and often, traveling from plant to plant in his ancient Ford. But unless you are a retired person of means or someone without family obligations, spending your time in such an unstructured way is not an efficient method for gathering exclusive investment information. There are more valuable and well-structured approaches to sleuthing, as you'll soon see.

Before we proceed, let me again reiterate the following important point: You should not enlist moles, nor should you aim to be invited into the company's offices in order to peek at confidential documents or hear confidential conversations by insiders, nor should you do any other thing that the law forbids. Later I'll list other actions you cannot take, but for the time being let's simply say that whenever you have any doubt about an action, you should consult your lawyer. Keep a record of your questions—verbatim, if you can, including the time and date—then take careful notes of what your attorney tells you—again, verbatim, plus the time and the date. You will likely not need most of these records, but on the off-chance that you do, they will be indispensable.

I'm not being overly cautious. As I said before, some information you find by physical sleuthing may later seem prescient to others, so proving that you obtained it legitimately might make all the difference between enjoying your gains and being in trouble. The following example makes this point more vividly.

EXTERNAL SURVEILLANCE AND A CRUCIAL PRECAUTION

Say it's the late 1980s and you read in a New York magazine an interview with the founder of a famed leveraged buyout firm, in which the man said that at his firm, lunches and breakfasts were for routine matters while dinners were reserved for final deals, where nothing but the best French food was catered. Because your mind works like that of a sleuth, fixing on *physical* details, you promptly ask your assistant to call all the French restaurants in town, telling them you are looking for the best caterer for a very important corporate dinner. She is to request corporate references. Within three days she finds the restaurant that caters for the LBO firm. You then pay her extra to park each evening in front of the midtown brownstone that serves as the LBO firm's headquarters. After a few fruitless nights observing the building, she phones in and tells you that the French caterer's van has arrived at the brownstone and men in toques are offloading provisions.

You thank her, call your lawyers to notify them of your actions, jot down a memo-to-file, and stamp it with the date and time by the trading room's time clock. (Today you'd send an e-mail to yourself or to your lawyer, which would time-stamp it.) You then pick up your camera with the telephoto lens, and in half an hour you join your assistant in her car. As you wait, you photograph the caterer's van several times (each photo is dated and time-stamped), and by six o'clock your wait is rewarded. You see seven men in suits arriving and being received warmly at the brownstone's doorstep by the LBO's two senior partners. You snap a dozen photographs of them, and, for good measure, your assistant snaps a few more on her own camera. You both take notes and initial them, marking the time as the notes are made. You also initial each other's notes for good measure. Then you wait some more, and just before midnight the brownstone door opens and the seven men emerge. As the two senior LBO partners accompany the departing guests to two limos, shaking their hands effusively, you snap more pictures, and so does your assistant—especially insightful is the photo where all guests are seen smiling with satisfaction and triumph as they enter the limo and drive away.

Next day you develop the photographs. You take your legally obtained photos to your friendly headhunter, who for a standard per-hour fee identifies the photographed subjects as the chairman, the president, and two senior VPs of Poker-chip Enterprises, Inc., PEI's top in-house counsel, and two well-known New York lawyers specializing in buyouts. That very same morning you put in a buy order for call options on Poker-chip Enterprises' stock, on the reasonable supposition that PEI is about to be acquired. The buyout indeed takes place a week later, and you triple your money. All's well that ends well? Not quite. The following week you receive a barely polite phone call from the market surveillance committee of the New York Stock Exchange, whose compliance team had tracked to you the inordinately large option trade. Can you please explain, they ask, how you had obtained the information that led you to buy—fortuitously—several hundreds of thousands of dollars worth of call options, a mere week before the happy event?

Certainly, you say: "Here is the phone number of my attorney, who can explain in detail and provide documentation." And after that, you hear nothing further about the matter from the New York Stock Exchange.

Your prudence has pre-empted the charge of trading on inside information by proving that there was none. Everything you did was based on public information. *Physical* information, yes, but *public* just the same.

If, instead of taking precautions, you had sat alone in your car, taken no pictures or notes, and had merely identified the departing execs by sight, then bought the call options, your goose might have been cooked because you could not prove you had obtained the information legally. But the photos have a time and date stamp. Your assistant was with you in the car and could provide supporting testimony, if necessary. You had told your lawyer the day before what you were planning, she had okayed it, and both of you took notes of the conversation, which were time-stamped. Your conversation with the lawyer was recorded. You had not used the photographs for blackmail, nor had you or anyone tied to you done anything illegal. Certainly parking on a public street and taking photographs in a public place is perfectly legal. In sum, all your actions have been legal, and the legality had been perfectly documented. After your lawyer provides all this evidence to the authorities, they quietly drop the matter.

They drop it, first, because they have no grounds for any action. But second, and more interestingly, because it is not in their interest to give other investors the idea to engage in physical spying on companies—even in public spaces.

SLEUTHS INVEST ON PHYSICAL EVIDENCE

Did such things happen? In the 1980s when LBOs were popular, certain similar cases are indeed rumored to have taken place, to have been investigated by the authorities, but to have gone unpublicized so as not to give ideas to the general public. Because, as you are presumably beginning to realize, for 99 percent of the population—the authorities included—"information" is what one gets from documents containing letters and numbers over which the companies and most often the authorities have control. The very idea of gathering *physical* information for private use, at the expense of those who don't garner that physical information, is something very few even consider.

So again—and I hope now you understand why I repeat this—take notes of whatever you do, consult your lawyer routinely, take notes of your consultations, make sure you have witnesses for activities that generate physical information, and always act as if one day you'll have to prove you did nothing wrong, because one day when you make a lot of money by sleuthing, you may very well have to.

The cost of consulting a lawyer routinely can be expensive, but you should consider such costs an integral part of sleuthing. Legal expense, by the way, is tax deductible, as are travel and phone expenses for sleuthing, if properly documented. In the same way that the CIA has integrated legal advice into its operations to keep its personnel out of jail, so should you.

IN-COMPANY INFORMATION GATHERING

Not all corporate sleuthing takes place in big cities. Many publicly traded companies are headquartered in midsize and small towns. No matter where you live, I'll bet that within 50 miles of your home there are at least a dozen offices of public companies. Just call your town's chamber of commerce and they'll provide you with a list. Besides, a corporate headquarters is not the only location worth sleuthing. Equally worthy are the company's plants, warehouses, and transportation hubs, which can be at other physical locations. Furthermore, a large part of people-sleuthing is observation and surveillance of company personnel in diners, restaurants, bars, and other public places, not just their natural corporate habitat. To meet corporate personnel in such public places, you have to show initiative and either eavesdrop or join the groups, if you are comfortable with this. It is easier, however, to penetrate the company physically by being invited.

For example, let's assume you manage to convince the investor relations manager to give you a tour of the premises. Or perhaps at the annual meeting you met the corporate accountant, with whom you struck up a quick friendship because you are both fly fishermen, or NASCAR enthusiasts, or Penn State grads (all of which information you could have learned through the Internet). Anything else will do equally well. Just get invited in. And once you're in, you can begin to get a measure of the company's key people, both as *individuals* and as a *group*.

EVALUATING INDIVIDUALS

Freud said that people drip secrets from their fingertips. What he meant was that everything people do and say reveals their character, wants, fears, and values. For example, scan the company's parking lot. If the executive slots are marked, see what the CEO drives. A turbocharged Porsche with a license plate that reads TOP DOGG? Or a 15-year-old Caddy, lovingly restored, with the license plate GZMO MKR? Does the CFO drive a sober Ford, or a red open-topped Fiat Spider with license plate CRTV ACT? Do other cars look new and clean, indicating a well-paid and meticulous workforce? Or are cars old and dilapidated? Is the front yard full of weeds and one letter in the corporate logo missing? Or is everything spic-and-span and the logo affectionately buffed? Note everything and anything for later reference.

Once inside, look around you. Is the reception area decorated with samples of the company's award-winning widgets and the CEO's patent certificates, or with pictures of the CEO meeting movie stars and foreign leaders? In the first case, he serves the company; in the second, the company serves him. Which company would you rather invest in?

As you are being led in to meet your newly made friend, keep looking around. How would you describe the people you meet on the way? Happy? Busy? Or surly? Let all your senses open up and gather impressions to be processed later. Note any details that, if chosen by a novelist to describe his characters, would add to your understanding of employees' personalities. Make a habit of picking up the magazines spread out on the table in the lobby or in waiting areas near executive offices, and search for the name on the subscription page. Does the CEO subscribe to *Widgets World*? Or is his name on *Town and Country* magazine? In the first case his mind is likely on the product; in the second case, on social climbing. (Unless the company sells high-class furniture to the town-and-country set, in which case the latter magazine would of course be a professional necessity.) As for the CFO, is his name on *Accounting World* or on *Yachting World*? Or even, heaven forbid, on *Gaming International*?

What you are looking for is signs of people's motivation. These, and signs of their ability, will give you deeper insight into your chances of making money via this stock. Let's start with what makes these people tick—their motivation.

EVALUATING MOTIVATION

Motivation comes in two types—external and internal. External employee motivation is often called *incentive* and flows from wages, bonuses, promotion chances, and other structures put in place to ensure that corporate individuals are pulling in one direction. To determine an employee's level of external motivation, you should find out how much each key person earns as well as how much that individual's bonus is tied to his or her own performance, and how much is tied to the corporation's overall performance via stock options. You, of course, would like to know if a key individual also purchased stock in the market with his or her after-tax money. Stock purchases and options are public information (see Appendix A for sources of this information), but the wages and bonuses have to be checked out elsewhere. Investor relations can often give you this information, if you ask, or you may inquire directly with the executives. Some may tell, others won't. Some headhunters can tell you what the standard rate in the industry is, or you can search the Internet for this information. This kind of motivation structure may not vary much within an industry, but you should endeavor to find out the details just the same.

The other kind of motivation—the internal kind—is often more important for your purposes but harder to discern. Parts of it can be gleaned from the person's background and accomplishments, most of which are public information, and more can be picked up from the person's dress, speech, and manner, as well as his or her surroundings. This is one of the main reasons you'd like to be invited inside a company, where you can take a look at the executives' offices and survey the mementos on the wall, which indicate what they consider to be important. For example, is the prominent photograph behind the CEO's desk a picture of the CEO beaming next to a happy client upon delivery of the latest gizmo?

Or is he photographed next to his yacht? And is the CFO photographed alongside his loving wife and four children, for whom he likely toils ceaselessly? Or does his wall sport a flashy Polaroid photo from the company's latest strategy session in the Las Vegas Playboy Club, where he is being embraced by three voluptuous bunnies?

You may say such matters are irrelevant because people are entitled to their private lives. You are right about the second part, but wrong about the first. Everything is relevant to stock sleuths—everything. The choices people make in their public displays, either in their clothing, trophies, personal mannerisms, choice of words, cars, or topics of conversation, can teach you a lot about their personality and values. If you are about to entrust your family's savings to strangers, you should first find out everything you can about these individuals—but then keep what you find to yourself. Do not gossip; do not tarnish other people's reputations. Do keep in mind how my Stanford biz team kept Company A President's misadventure secret from the class, as related in the Introduction. I would suggest that you be equally careful about repeating information you gather regarding people at the companies you sleuth.

There are at least three reasons for such circumspection. First, diminishing others to enhance your own stature is morally reprehensible. Second, if you tell tales about past informants, future informants will likely shy away from you. But third, and most practical, if you blurt out hard-sleuthed information, you are hurting yourself directly by providing sellers with reasons not to sell to you, and potential buyers with reasons not to buy what you have to sell. Just imagine what would have happened if the stock sleuth from the earlier LBO story had boasted of his discovery to his friends at the neighborhood bar. Not only would he be mocking the LBO company about its lax security so that next time acquisition candidates would arrive at the back or meet at an anonymous hotel, but he would be robbing his family of well-deserved gains, by giving them to strangers who might bid up the price of the call options he would like to buy.

Remember, if you find evidence of character flaws in company personnel, flaws in a company's operations, or anything else that may embarrass either the company or its people, keep the findings in mind for your own decision-making purposes, but keep that information to yourself.

EVALUATING GROUP INTERACTION

The character and motivation of a company's people tell sleuths only half the story. The other half of the story is told by how these individuals interact with each other as a group, and how effective they are as a team. You can often find this out simply by seeing the group in action. Who talks to whom, who treats others with disdain, who seems to be the natural leader (it is not always the CEO), who seems subservient, who provides ideas, and who vets them. Any company event you can get yourself invited to can provide such an opportunity, be it formal or informal. One of my preferred tactics is to chat with company personnel in their favorite lunchtime spots. I once received very frank feedback about a certain CEO of a large technology company in Silicon Valley from a group of top engineers lunching at the Main Street diner in the small town where the company was headquartered. From the blunt comments it was clear that the CEO's support in the company was dwindling fast, as most engineers saw her as a self-aggrandizing superstar using the company to generate more fame for herself, rather than using her name and access to open doors for the company's products. Whether their comments were fair or not was not the issue—they reflected near unanimity in the company's engineering ranks, as was confirmed by similar conversations with other company personnel in other eating spots. We followed up with further sleuthing, shorted the stock, and made money when the CEO was ousted.

Besides such external gatherings, the next-best indicator for team interaction is office layout—who sits where. Proximity to the CEO gives one clout, and also indicates where the CEO's heart is. If the R&D vice president sits closest to the CEO, maybe the CFO wouldn't have much sway in cutting the R&D budget. If the marketing vice president sits closest, sales expenses are probably more secure. If the CFO sits nearest to the boss, the company may be run by the book; yet if the main task is to come up with new products, the probability of success may be less than what the foolish money believes, especially if the sales vice president sits far away from the R&D chief, so their day-to-day interaction is infrequent.

Of course, physical layout is not absolute proof of anything, but it is one more data point that outsiders don't have. And if conclusions drawn from it are supported by other physical evidence, they are likely to give you an edge. (In the case noted above, we found that the CEO surrounded herself physically with a team of public relations experts.)

In general, I find it a useful habit to observe everything and everyone during a company visit, keep my eyes and ears open, and make mental notes; then once I am back in my car, do a "brain-dump" and write down in an unstructured fashion any details that pop into my mind without pausing to reflect upon their importance. Only later in my office do I analyze them, both alone and in concert with assistants, partners, and advisors.

ANALYSIS BY YOUR SLEUTHING PARTNERS

Having partners and advisors is very important for a stock sleuth at this stage. In intelligence operative circles, such discussions about individuals and interaction of "the opposing team" often take place in safe houses or safe rooms, where your own team members are holed up before an operation and have time to hash out the newly discovered evidence and its potential implications. Similarly, in stock sleuthing, it helps if you have someone trustworthy with whom to discuss your findings—a spouse, a trusted partner, or, if you are a member of an investment club or a money management team, team members who can pick out from your brain-dump notes further important implications that you had missed.

Here are some typical questions your sleuthing partners should attempt to answer about the opposing team:

What are the strengths and weaknesses of each member of the company team, based on the evidence?

Is the team structured to achieve the necessary aims?

How well do these people work together? Are they all pulling in the same direction, or do their individual goals diverge? Why? Is it because of badly structured incentives? Or because of conflicting ambitions?

What are the internal tensions?

What factions or coalitions are there?

Every work group with a common goal—be it a corporation, a lever-aged-buyout partnership, a sports team, a hit squad, or the security team defending the hit target—is composed of individual actors whose actions cannot be generalized and expressed in numbers and math only. Any team constitutes a human drama in progress where individual actors are of key importance. If you invest in a company without knowing anything about its own specific drama, or characters, you'll likely end up losing your money to stock sleuths who do.

If you're concerned that the techniques used to find such information are too hard for an amateur, think again. Most of what I'm suggesting is doable by anyone—no experience necessary, just willingness to try, normal common sense, and an adventurous spirit. Only about one-tenth of the techniques described here require some experience, and you don't have to try them all at once. Just pick whatever techniques seem most suitable to your skills and personality and simplify them to suit your taste and time constraints. As your experience and self-confidence grow (often a direct result of making money by sleuthing), even what at first seemed daunting will become easy, and soon you'll even start modifying the methods described here and inventing your own techniques. To help you understand how to blend together all you've learned. I'll walk you through the sleuthing process using one specific case.

BACKGROUND AND STATUS EVALUATIONS

Say you had found a Midwestern company—XYZ Enterprises—with a future that seems bright and a stock price you consider very cheap, and thus worth sleuthing. (Chapter 7 will give you a few tips on how to pick such potentially good stocks.) Your first step is to run a background check on the management team. The investor relations department can provide much of this, and the rest you can find on the Internet or by talking to past colleagues of the executives, if you are comfortable phoning around.

Say you find that all three top execs graduated from Stanford Biz 15 years ago. Two worked for a large brokerage firm located in a metropolitan area as investment bankers for 13 years, while the third joined the

Midwestern company founded by his father, where he became CEO. Two years ago he recruited his two classmates to help run the company. The personal background of these two recent-joiners? While at the brokerage firm, the two men were members of the Yacht Club and engaged in fly-fishing in Vermont and skeet-shooting in their firm's exclusive country-side camp. The CEO, on the other hand, likes NASCAR racing, competes in lake-fishing contests, and hunts moose. So two high-status, high-earning professional underlings with aristocratic pursuits have now joined a boss who inherited his father's company ready-made, and whose own tastes favor more common hobbies. If you don't think these differences matter, read Paul Fussell's book *Class: A Guide to the American Status System* (as noted in Appendix A, a must-read for any North American stock sleuth).

ESTABLISH MOTIVATION

With the executives' background researched, both external and internal motivations can be addressed. Why did the two investment bankers join XYZ Enterprises? A higher salary is one possible reason. Another possible reason may be that their careers stalled or that they got tired of the big city rat race and wanted to relax in the Midwest. It's unlikely that two such status-minded urban strivers moved without strong motivation into what for them must seem like a backwater community, after they had rubbed shoulders with the elite. But what if both originally came from small towns too, so, for them, going to XYZ really meant going back to their roots? Of course other reasons may exist—say both served with the CEO in Vietnam as common grunts and have become blood brothers, so when he asked them to come help him rescue his family business, they could not say no. If so, perhaps you should try to find out whether they know his father, too. The more you know, the better your chances of making a wise investment choice.

BACKGROUND AND CHARACTER ASSESSMENTS

Finding the information on background and character goes to the heart of the sleuthing method. You have to ask those who know the execs, then combine those details with the slivers of information you obtained from other informants and published sources in order to form a mental picture of the executives' personalities. The Internet provides some formal background of executives (see sources in Appendix A) and also of mid-level managers (who may have their names and telephone numbers on product announcements). People's names appear on directors' lists of sports clubs, hobby competitions, university graduation rosters, and much more. You only have to Google them, and occasionally follow up with phone calls.

Another option is to pay an executive search consultant—a headhunter—to get specialized information for you. Such professionals cost money, just as lawyers do, but in the case of potentially large investments, they are worth their fee. Remember, if your portfolio has only four or five stock investments, every bit of real-life information about the human drama into which you intend to sink your family's hard-earned savings is important. After all, if you planned to buy the entire company, this is what you'd do, wouldn't you? Well then, if you intend to use a substantial portion of your savings to buy a part of the company, shouldn't you do the same? And just as XYZ's CEO would not dream of doing all the research himself, so should you get into the habit of paying for experienced, competent help in gathering key information. Because the more you know, the better your chances are to make money on the investment—and those chances are enhanced by *not* investing in whatever makes you uneasy or uncomfortable. As you'll find out quickly enough, the "no go" decisions are often as important as the "go" decisions. Recall that Warren Buffett's first rule of investing is "Don't lose money." The more you know about the company's human element, the better your chances of following Buffett's first rule.

FIND YOUR OWN PREFERRED METHOD

S uch information gathering does not come easy to everyone. Nevertheless, you can train yourself to sniff out informal information about people's background and character. You will eventually find your own preferred methods and sources. Each stock sleuth develops his or her own approach: some prefer informal conversations, others more formal meetings.

My own preference is to get information by phone. I'm always afraid that when I meet people in person they may clam up or become cautious if they sense I am a significant investor. But over the phone, I find that perfect strangers often tell me things they would not tell their grandmothers. Whether it's my voice or my manner, I am not sure, but it works for me. Your own skills may run in different directions. Only you can find out what they are.

Which professional backgrounds are best for a stock sleuth, for digging out personal information? In my experience, the careers most suited for such digging are brokers used to cold calling, salespeople who have learned how to interact with newly met strangers and ask about their needs, seasoned police detectives, lawyers who have learned to pose questions mildly and sympathetically, human resources personnel, psychologists, and, in general, anyone who is genuinely fascinated by other people. (The last category includes me.) If you convey interest in others, people will open up to you to a surprising degree.

THE WORLD IS YOUR SLEUTHING OYSTER

S o who can you call for information? I prefer local chambers of commerce in the town where the company is headquartered, as well as bank managers, reporters at the local free weekly paper (they often know everything), personnel at area universities—anyone who is a member of the local community who will talk to me. I only have to say I am a pension fund manager (which I am), and it seems almost a public duty to help me. If they don't have the information, they usually know someone who knows someone else who does. I mainly do this by phone, but 10 to

20 percent of the time I visit sources in person and get acquainted with them. (Sleuthing the personal background of these individuals beforehand often helps.) Because most people do not get enough personal attention and you provide a sympathetic ear, they'll often tell you all they know. Can the skill of getting information be learned? Yes. Is it time consuming? Yes. Is it easy to do? No—and luckily so, because *the harder the information is to get, the likelier it will be exclusive to you.* This is because the foolish money rarely takes the trouble to sleuth.

Let's go back to XYZ's newly hired executives. Before you meet them in person, you should draft a list of hypotheses about their motivations for joining. There are some obvious ones, such as ambition. Yes, they were members of the Yacht Club, but at the brokerage firm they took orders from the CEO; maybe they joined XYZ in the hopes of rising quickly to the C-level ranks themselves.

What if higher salaries were the enticement? That could be, but unless their careers have stalled badly (which you should check), it is unlikely the two would have joined for mere higher wages; a partner in a large investment bank makes at least as much as a Midwestern CEO. (Be sure of this by checking with your friendly headhunter or researching compensation surveys on the Internet.) Certainly the social status of a senior partner is at least as high as that of a Midwestern CEO. (Or is it really? Check this out, too.)

It is also possible that, besides the chance to be a chief executive, if not the new CEO, the two have left the big city and joined XYZ because they see it as a great growth opportunity, where they can make far more in stock options than in banking bonuses. This growth opportunity, in fact, is one of the reasons you had zeroed in on the company initially—two highly paid, talented execs at the peak of their careers, betting their futures on the opportunity here. How can you confirm this assumption? A simple perusal of their salaries and option grants given in the annual information circular will usually do. If you find that they had accepted a modest salary, but a very large grant of options, this would suggest that they are very bullish on XYZ. It doesn't mean you'd automatically buy the stock, but it would mean that it's worthwhile to continue your sleuthing. It would also mean that the internal human dynamics would be less important, because a high potential payoff often aligns conflicting interests. You might then go directly to researching the customers, the product, and the plant and periphery.

But assume you have found that the two new arrivals have more wages than options, implying that growth prospects are only moderate (which you still have to verify by sleuthing the customers and the product), yet the stock is very cheap. Other questions would now arise, such as competition between the two execs over the CEO's job, which now appears to be the main reason they joined. It may be friendly or bitter, and if the latter, might influence XYZ's ability to obtain more checks from its customers. And how would your conclusion change if you learned that the CEO's son also works at XYZ? He's the assistant vice president of sales with the clammy handshake you met at the annual meeting, and who, despite his lowly rank, sits in on all meetings (this you learned from the receptionist he has tried to paw) and is likely being groomed for a top job.

If that last bit is true, it might nix your investment. However, what if the CEO's son is an idiot (you have to cross-check this, because the receptionist's opinion may be biased), and that's why the CEO brought in the two Stanford alums? One of these two may be much older, and thus a temporary mentor for the CEO's son, while the second is meant to be CEO. In such a case, you may still invest. But what if the son is really brilliant?

Do not doubt that these questions are relevant. They go to the heart of the workings of any check-receiving work group, and cannot be captured by Sharpe's risk/reward ratios, Merton's formula for risk, correlation coefficients, price charts with exponential moving averages, or even financial analysis. The questions involve the personalities of the main players, motivations, environment, the interaction of these elements, and the physical details that point to them. In searching for the answers, you go through a process similar to that of actors or writers who load themselves with details about the characters in their stories, their backgrounds, and motivations, until a magic transformation takes place—the characters come alive, and there is an instinctive knowledge of where the story is going, and whether the characters are likely to succeed or fail.

PHYSICAL INFORMATION AND HUMAN COMMUNICATION CHANNELS VERSUS SYMBOLS

The processing of physical, human information described above is entirely missing in the mathematical theory of finance—indeed, the efficient market theory is oblivious to the existence of such data (and luckily so, for the sleuths among us).

My goal is to show you how to get exclusive *information* about a *company*, in order to invest profitably. I started by asking what a *company* is, and said it's a check-receiving work group (made up of physical elements you can sleuth firsthand). So now the next logical question is: What is *information*? For most investors, information is strictly symbols—numbers and letters gathered by others and transmitted via print media or the Internet, which you can analyze to decide what to buy and what to sell.

In real life, however, we humans receive (and transmit) a great deal of information not as symbols but physically and directly, via our five senses. Of these senses, sight and sound predominate even though the other three also channel information. (For example, the alcoholic breath and the clammy handshake of the assistant VP of sales, whom you later learn is the CEO's son.) But even the two dominant senses are used by most investors only for receiving *secondhand* information—printed matter or blips on computer screens—via words and numbers that serve only as *models* of the real company. But they do not capture even a small part of the *physical* details relevant to investment decision making.

But just how necessary and relevant to investment information are primary, physical sensations? This question is inextricably tied to several other questions: How important is the *human* part of a company to your successful investment in its stock? How much do you lose if you view the stock in terms of numbers only, as indexers do? And how far can you generalize specific human behavior—or, indeed, human drama, which is what commerce really is? Can you analyze behavior only with mathematics?

The assumption that human behavior can be captured entirely via symbols is a deeply flawed one. In physics and mathematics it led to seeming paradoxes that, for thousands of years, seemed unassailable. The Greek Zeno concocted a paradox that proved in math the impossibility of all motion, since moving across any distance would first necessitate moving across half of it (and before that, moving across half *that*, and so on ad infinitum). More recently, in the mid-twentieth century, the physicist Erwin Schroedinger showed the math of quantum mechanics led to considering a cat as both dead and alive simultaneously. And, more recently still, in the field of investments, efficient market theorists came up with the famous million coin-flipping monkeys, 10 of whom were shown to be "statistical" investment geniuses after 10 years of flipping, even though their results could be declared random.

The early paradoxes have a direct bearing on stock sleuthing, because the thinking behind them is very much like the mathematical reasoning that led to index funds—the foolish money you are trying to take by sleuthing. The paradoxes were perplexing because they made the assumption that if something is true in the mathematical equation (or in language or in logic, which is also a sort of mathematics) used to describe reality, it must be true in reality as well.

During the last 50 years, however, scientists have begun to understand that this is false. Math has some properties the world doesn't have, and vice versa. Math is only a map of the world, as is language. Thus, Zeno's paradox is known today to be bogus, just like the paradox of Schroedinger's cat. The first made the assumption that if math is smooth (there is always a point between two others), so is the world. But that is not true. The world is lumpy, or as physicists say, "discrete." Thus, real physical movement is possible, and the paradox vanishes. As for Schroedinger's cat—just because human math says something, it doesn't obligate the cat in any way. In both these cases (and in others), what math said was fine for math, but not for the world. Indeed, a colleague of Einstein named Kurt Goedel showed that the entire symbolic representation of reality has inherent limitations. (As noted in Appendix A, the excellent book—*Goedel's Proof*, by Ernest Nagel and James R. Newman— explains Goedel's findings.)

You may be wondering about the relevance of all this to investing. The connection is direct, since it impacts hundreds of billions of dollars of index funds. While it is now widely accepted that math has severe limitations in capturing reality, in the world of investments billions are still invested based only on printed symbolic echoes of the intense human drama that is commerce, without ever going to the physical source! This amounts to implicitly accepting the assumption that such symbolic echoes of commerce contain all of what investors need—an assumption proven wrong in other areas of human knowledge-seeking, yet still foolishly followed in investing.

Let me say this again. If you invest based only on paper printouts and screen information, you (like my old biz school classmates) must be assuming that the symbolic echoes of commercial conflict (which is what business competition truly is) are enough to tell you which side in the commercial conflict is stronger, which is weaker, which tells the truth, which lies, which can deliver, and which cannot.

But are symbolic echoes of human activity really sufficient for this?

WHAT DOES IT MEAN TO BE HUMAN?

You may not realize it, but this question is 70 years old. In its early incarnation, the question was, "Do symbols and language suffice to tell you whether a respondent tells the truth—indeed, whether the respondent is human at all?" This, in short, is the *Turing Test*, which was named after Alan Turing, the British mathematical genius who helped break the German secret code in World War II. Because Turing's hidden assumption is extremely important for our sleuthing purposes, let's say a few words about it, before going back to XYZ Enterprises.

Alan Turing proposed the following scenario: You are sitting in front of a wall with a slot in it, into which you can slide pieces of paper with your written questions, and from which you receive written answers in return—in English (or in any other language for that matter, including computer code). There is an entity behind the wall that answers your questions in the same language, or code, but whether the entity is a human or a computer programmed to answer like one, you don't know. Note that the entity can be a clever artificial intelligence computer that sometimes lies and sometimes tells the truth, like humans do, or a clever human that simulates a mechanical computer by giving only mechanical stupid answers.

Turing's famous question was: "Can you tell strictly *by the written answers* whether the hidden entity is human or not?" In other words, could you recognize the entity's humanness strictly by its *written* answers?

Compared to what we as sleuths want to know, Turing's question is the easy one. It asks only whether the hidden entity is human or not. It does not go into the question of whether the entity is a trustworthy human or a corrupt one, and, if it is an honest human, whether that human can deliver on his or her promises—which is what a stock sleuth would be concerned with. These are higher-order problems that the Turing Test cannot even remotely address—its own simple question is hard enough to answer as it is.

So what is the answer? It may interest you to learn that, to this day, Turing's question has not been answered conclusively. But, as you'll also see below, just like Zeno's paradox, Turing's Test, too, proves to be bogus.

To see why, we must focus on the second part of the Turing Test, which received less notice. In that second part, Turing specified that, for purposes of answering his question, you are not allowed to peek behind the wall or speak to the entity behind it. All interactions between you and the entity are to be done solely via typed notes.

This is an extremely important limitation, with a direct bearing on index fund investors, and all those who invest based only on mathematical information and corporate filings obtainable through the Internet. Because Turing's injunction not to peek behind the wall implies an obvious assumption—that it is extremely hard, indeed perhaps impossible, for a machine to simulate human behavior when the human tester perceives the tested entity *directly* and *physically*. To trick the observer in such a direct encounter, we'd have to construct an android that looks and acts like a human—not only on paper, but in physical life. That's why Turing's Test is not really a test, but an admission that *full human communications cannot be achieved via language (or symbols) alone*—which is all that computers can work with.

Computers cannot flirt, raise an eyebrow, roll their eyes, twitch uncomfortably when caught in a lie, or blush. They cannot shake your hand, exchange meaningful glances with other computers, or convey the many other nonverbal cues that humans use in commercial activities, and which help those who provide capital decide whether they should invest in these activities.

This, in a nutshell, is why stock sleuths can take index fund investors' money. The latter only get the written notes through the Internet screen while the former can "peek behind the screen," and look (and hear, smell, and feel) the physical company behind the screen—its people, product, plant, and periphery.

(And in case you were wondering about the investing monkeys: Warren Buffett had a famously sly counterargument to that paradox: What if you found that seven of the ten remaining simians all lived in Omaha, Nebraska? . . . Wouldn't you at least be curious to learn what kind of bananas they ate? i.e.: What physical "inputs" they used? . . .)

And now we can return to XYZ.

MESSAGES FROM BEYOND TURING'S WALL

Assume you read in a press release on the Internet that XYZ's VP of sales had said, "We think the coming year's sales will be good." Since this is a formal statement by the company, you become more bullish on the stock. Right?

Imagine, however, that instead of just reading the statement's words, you actually *saw* and *heard* the sales VP say this *in person*: you noticed his tone of voice and the emphasis he put on the word "think," and you also saw him twist his mouth and raise one eyebrow at the same time. Would it make a difference to your conclusion? Sure would, because much of the crucial information was lost when the communication was condensed into printed symbols. Quite clearly, then, investment conclusions you'd reach from the mere reading of reports on the Internet, versus what you'd conclude from a direct contact, *based on the same words*, could be diametrically opposed.

Now, answer this question: If you limited yourself to investing *only* in stocks where you could receive information physically and directly from the key players whom you took the trouble to get to know personally (peeking over Turing's wall, as it were), while other investors only read the legally approved corporate messages via words on the screen (Turing's wall slot, as it were), who do you think would take whose money over the long term? Even if those other investors listened to the occasional corporate conference calls and got some of the voice nuances, so much else would be lost to them that no analysis of the publicly reported data would help.

CONGRUENT AND INCONGRUENT COMMUNICATION

Yet this is only the beginning: There's far more to direct human communications than even the full richness of a single channel, be it sight or sound. Humans do not transmit information, rich as it may be, over a single channel. Rather, they transmit it over several channels simultaneously—they speak, gesture, move their faces, sniff, twitch, look sideways, and much more—they practically *perform* as they communicate.

When all human physical transmission channels convey the same message, the communication is called *congruent*. When different channels convey different messages, the communication is called *incongruent*.

If you are physically present when a live person delivers a message—if you peek over Turing's wall—you get the full content on all channels, and you can better determine if it is congruent or not. Furthermore, if the information is being given by a group, the performance then becomes communal, the number of channels rises severalfold, and the number of possible incongruent dissonances increases manyfold.

EVERYONE CAN IDENTIFY INCONGRUENT MESSAGES

The ability to identify incongruent human messages is innate to all humans as a matter of survival. Even if you have little expertise in business, if you had witnessed XYZ's incongruent message face-to-face, you'd likely say something like, "I saw and heard the VP speak, but something didn't seem quite right. I don't know what, I don't know why, but somehow I don't believe what he said. Call it gut feeling." And so you don't buy the stock—and likely you save yourself and your family from a hefty loss.

Is your gut feeling then a legitimate stock research tool?

You better believe it. Your "gut feelings" are often the sum total of all your perceptions, after your brain processes and compares all messages for congruence. Your subconscious compares the tone of voice, the word emphasis, the voice quaver, the hemming and hawing, to judge whether all the channels said the same thing; whether parts of the communication conveyed opposing messages; whether the raised eyebrow, twisted lips, shifty eyes reinforced the message or weakened it. If the VP of sales in the above example sat among other execs as he spoke, what were their reactions to his words? Did they nod in agreement, or did they sit frozen-faced in silence as the assistant VP snorted in derision and sipped his vodka?

All of us receive parallel messages from other people on a daily basis, and we have learned to form judgments about their congruence, so as to know whom to trust, whom to believe, whom to employ, and whom to keep away from. These decisions are most likely not made by our neurons—our so-called gray matter—but rather, by the liquid limbic system that feeds the brain in ways not completely understood. (Not that our neural decision making is completely understood either.) We do not always make the right decisions, of course. To err is human. But, luckily, it is also human to face our limitations and to compensate for them. This is why most people, before making important decisions about others, prefer to meet them face-to-face, to give all their own senses and all parts of their brain a chance to have an input into the decision making.

See also Malcolm Gladwell's book, *Blink* (noted in Appendix A), for some wonderful examples and elaboration on the topic of instinctive human decision making, based on direct sensory input.

Unfortunately, when your sensory input is limited, you can get suckered. The probability of making wrong decisions rises when we carelessly let ourselves be fed information through a single channel, and allow our other channels to be blocked—again à la Turing: An unknown broker with a seductive voice calls with a hot tip that must be seized immediately, and so we buy without bothering to first visit his office (which, we later learn, is in a second-floor walkup next to the Salvation Army's soup kitchen). Or we buy an attractive ring cheaply off the TV, forgoing direct purchase in a store that would have let us feel the thinness of the metal and smell the acidity of the cheap patina. Or we embark on a week's vaca-tion in downtown Ouagadougou, since the hotel's pool in the photo seemed nice, and neglect to Google the town's name to learn of the civil war in progress.

Many poor decisions can be prevented if we engage more of our senses in the decision making, giving a chance for our healthy pang of unease to arise. And in matters of importance, bringing in five or ten more opin-ions to supplement our five senses is wise. In fact, you can safely assume that any time you are pressed to make an investment decision based on a single-channel input, and are dissuaded from using your other senses to gather *physical* information or from consulting others for their "sense" of the situation, you should let the investment go. There will always be oth-ers. Remember Warren Buffett's first rule of investing.

EXTRACTION OF INFORMATION FROM PHYSICAL EVIDENCE

The information you can get in a face-to-face meeting is often key. The CIA, which is one organization that has dedicated much thought and resources to the art of gathering information, is rumored to give its agents a course loosely called Extraction of Information from Physical Evidence (EIPE), known colloquially as Cold Reading 101. A similar course is rumored to be given to Mossad agents. The agents learn to scan the person they meet, make assumptions on the fly about his or her background, motivation, values, and personality traits, and then try to refute or confirm the assumptions via conversational tests. Jury selection consultants often use similar methods, though in a more formal setting.

The purpose of this type of information gathering is twofold: first, to understand the other person, and, second, to present yourself as a similar person in whose company the target would feel comfortable. There are even physical aspects to making the other person feel comfortable with you, either on the phone or in person, and there is a whole body of liter-ature about the topic. Similar courses for salespeople are taught by a cadre of American entrepreneurs—in a much reduced version and with different aims in mind—on the complexities of human interaction (called Social Dynamics and NLP, or Neuro Linguistic Programming). The Stasi, East Germany's intelligence service, used to teach its male agents (called Romeos) these techniques, to help them pick up Western secretaries in order to get inside information about their employers. The KGB used to teach its female agents (called Swallows) similar tricks, to entrap foreign diplomats. Whether the CIA teaches its personnel something similar is unknown, but it has been rumored that the Mossad trains both male and female intelligence agents in these skills. It may surprise you, but few of these skills have anything to do with sex. Most skills involve focusing attention on the other person, extracting values, forming hypotheses on the fly, sympathetic listening, and many other aspects of interactive cold reading. While the aims of intelligence agencies' cold readers and pick-up artists are different, the principles are similar.

COLD READING—AN EXERCISE

Let's say you met the VP of sales of XYZ Enterprises at the annual meeting and managed to chat with him. While you chit-chat, you apply your newly acquired skill of cold reading and notice the following details: The man is in his mid-fifties, stocky, healthy but with a double chin and a budding beer gut. He speaks in a Midwestern twang, using educated language but employing both football and golf metaphors, and the occasional Army simile. His hands are rough, but the nails well maintained. His belt buckle is made of cast iron embossed with a longhorn's head; his feet are shod in rodeo-style boots; his shirt made of good cotton checkered lightly. His face is sunburned and his mustache clipped. He has moderately long sideburns. His watch? A steel Rolex with three dials.

You probably already have a mental picture of him, and so can now formulate hypotheses, which your conversation can confirm or refute. What are his values? What does he consider important? What is unimportant? Whom is he trying to emulate in dress, manner, or speech? Is it a childhood hero, or an advertising icon? Or perhaps a TV or a movie personality? Whom is he trying to please? a harsh father? an elder brother? Why?

What are his ambitions? Is it merely to make a high bonus or to be known as the top salesman? Or perhaps to become CEO? If he'd made a million dollars, what would he do with it? Buy a longhorn cattle ranch? an airplane? a membership in a golf club? a timeshare in a jet? Would he retire? Or start a company? With whom? The CFO? The R&D VP? Are any of them buddies? And if so, how long? How did they meet? It suddenly occurs to you that the sales VP's values seem similar to the CEO's, but opposed to those of the two newly arrived execs. What does he think about them? Does he resent their arrival? If so, what is he likely to do? Will he leave? How important is this guy to XYZ? If he quit, would the CEO's idiot son become XYZ's sales VP? Or would one of the two new arrivals? And if so, how well could an urban skeet shooter who fancies yachting sell to XYZ's clients?

To learn the answers to the above is to be on the road to understanding which way XYZ is heading. And to make headway in this direction you must first understand the sales VP, perhaps befriend him, to extract information from him with the proviso that it cannot be inside information.

Do you feel like there are too many questions to ask? Or are they too deep? Too hard? These, and more, are the very basic questions any intelligence agent is trained to probe for when meeting a potential informant, so that he can defend his country. As the answers become clear, the agent can use them to gather more information from the informant—perhaps more than the informant thinks he's imparting.

In our case, assume that as you chat with the sales VP after the annual meeting, you form the hypothesis that as an outdoorsy kind of guy in his mid-fifties, with a military bearing and a military-style mustache and elocution, he may have served in the armed forces during the Vietnam War. You want to test this hypothesis because, if he had, that experience must have left an impression. (Remember the A-10 pilot I described in the Introduction, and how he came over to my side.) But even if you confirm that this indeed was the case, it might have left him with two opposing feelings—either instinctive obedience to authority or the opposite. You must probe to see which is correct before you can proceed. If it is the former and you convey authority in manner and nuance, he may automati-

cally open up to you. On the other hand, if it is the latter, you should convey the opposite, to get him to open up.

BUT IS IT ETHICAL?

I f you feel morally queasy about trying to befriend a stranger in such a
manner for personal gain, you shouldn't. First, remember you are
investing for your family. Just as you would defend them against
marauders, you should be willing to defend them against poverty by
befriending strangers to invest successfully on their behalf. But second,
the sales VP befriends people daily in order to persuade them to send
checks to XYZ, and he's doing it for his family. Why, then, should you
have qualms about doing the same to him, for yours?

So long as you take care not to get inside information, getting close to
company employees in order to get *physical* information from them is a
moral endeavor. Indeed, what can be more moral than learning as much
as you can about the group of strangers into whose hands you are about
to entrust your family savings? Yes, it does require that you leave your
office or home and that you go to meet people in the real world. And it
does necessitate some initiative and above average conversation skills,
along with the ability to listen sympathetically. But all of these skills are
healthy qualities that can make your family better off, as well as come in
handy in other areas of your life, be it work-related or personal.

If you still feel uneasy about penetrating the company and getting close
to its people, the next part should be easier for you—sleuthing the people outside the company who send the checks. These are the decision
makers among its customers.

GETTING TO KNOW THE COMPANY'S CUSTOMERS

My own techniques for sleuthing customers flow directly from the insights offered by those whose teaching stayed with me, particularly that of Steven Brandt, whom I studied with at Stanford University's Graduate School of Business, and Charlie Munger, Warren Buffett's legendary partner.

Of the biz school lessons that stayed with me for life, few were simpler than Steve Brandt's rule (following Peter Drucker's dicta) that everything flows from the customer, and that by asking four basic questions about a company's customers, you can gain a quick understanding of any business. Here are the four questions:

1. **WHO ARE THE CUSTOMERS?** Identify both the companies who buy your products and the people in those companies who make the purchase decisions.

2. **WHAT EXACTLY ARE THEY BUYING?** Clarify what is being purchased, both by the companies and by individuals within the companies.

3. **WHAT EXACTLY ARE YOU SELLING?** Clarify what you are selling both to the individual who makes the purchase decision and to his or her employer.

4. **WHY WOULD THEY BUY FROM YOU?** Clarify the reasons for their buying from you, again, both individually and as an organization.

If you find the answers to these four questions, they'll tell you nearly all you need to know about the business. The answers are often obvious, but other times they are not. Occasionally, they are unprintable. But if you want to make money in the stock, you simply must get true answers to all the questions.

Now a word of caution; these four questions will not tell you whether the customer is worth serving. Warren Buffett might ask, "Is it a good business?" Or, in my own formulation: Is this business worth doing?

In a shocking number of cases, the answer is a definite no. Just as some books are not worth reading, and some movies not worth watching, some businesses are not worth doing. The unworthiness of a business can be seen in a low return on investment, cyclicality, no control over costs, and other numerical equivalents of living in a one-horse town with nothing to do and no one to talk to while being forced to wash the dishes all day long for eleven siblings who never say thank-you. The details can vary, but the conclusion is the same: this business isn't worth doing.

HOBBIES MASQUERADING AS BUSINESSES

Want examples? There are plenty. The airline industry has never made a penny, collectively, since it started. Warren Buffett (whom I find I quote a lot here) said that the first moment the Wright brothers' plane flew, any honest capitalist should have shot it down to do a favor to all other capitalists. As an ex-aerospace engineer and an ex-model airplane champion, these words give me intense pain, but the capitalist part of me admits grudgingly that they are nevertheless true. Unions, international politics, heavy capital spending needs, and irrational competition for customers all combine to make the occupation of flying people hither and yon into a mere hobby. So if you want to analyze a cheap airline stock, be my guest, but unless it's a trading fling (which this book does not recommend), you are on your own and will probably be out of money very soon.

Similarly, North American car manufacturing today is a close cousin to the airline business (but not the airplane-making business, which is nearly a government-supported monopoly). With huge pension obligations and highly paid, high-girth employees competing with low-wage, low-girth employees in foreign lands, do not even bother to invest time sleuthing such companies.

Ditto some businesses selling complex systems to large banks. Bank employees have little decision-making power, so purchase decisions are made by a committee and take more than a year to make. Suppliers end up spending their shareholders' equity to finance the clients' bureaucracy. Well, not with my money they don't.

Can we say then that the sleuthing method works best for smaller companies? It's obvious that such businesses are easier to comprehend, the number of their key people is lower, and so are the numbers of their key products and key customers. But every now and then a larger company can also be a good target for sleuthing. The choice is up to you—so long as you keep the overarching question in mind: Is this business worth doing?

BUFFETT'S EVOLUTION

You will be surprised to learn that Warren Buffett had himself ignored this question at the beginning of his career. When he started investing, he only cared about buying stocks very cheaply, no matter what the business. In Buffett's own formulation, he was looking to buy three-puff cigar butts for the price of one puff, so as to sell them for two. This strategy was a fairly simple one, because it did not matter how good or how bad the company's clients were. Buffett was simply looking to buy *any* company at one-third of its "cadaver value," and sell it for double that.

The drawback to such cheap-stock investing was that Buffett had to keep finding more and more "three-puff butts," and keep buying them and selling them, all the while paying the taxes on his gains. Now, there's nothing wrong with paying tax on gains, of course. In my own money management company, we often say we'd like to give our clients as large a capital gains tax bill as we can. But the flaw in Buffett's early strategy was that it was based on the principle of "acting often"—like flying an acrobatic plane where you must be "on the controls" all the time. It was almost like day trading, though not as frequent, in that he did not really care what the company did, or how good its customers were, or how good the business. Since Buffett only wanted to own the stock for the duration of one puff, why should he have cared?

By the way, that's how Buffett came to own what later became the hub of his empire—Berkshire Hathaway, a New England cloth manufacturer with run-down machinery but with the twin advantages of generating free cash and selling below working capital.

ENTER CHARLIE MUNGER

Buffett's cheap-stock strategy changed when he partnered with Charlie Munger, a business lawyer trained in concepts and hierarchies of concepts. So while Buffett at that time focused on the numbers, Munger focused on the company's business quality and came up with a remarkable insight: Very few companies are really worth owning. The great majority are mediocre or worse. Buffett took his findings very much to heart, and he later said that every investor should limit himself to 20 investments in a lifetime. Only this way can he be sure not to waste time and money on the average and marginal. In my own firm we are not as restrictive, but we come close.

This view is not as extreme as it sounds. Many more companies waste their talent and resources on unworthy clients than those who serve good clients. It's as if Alan Greenspan became the in-house economist and investment advisor of a small brokerage firm in a tiny mining town. The town residents might be very happy to have him, but as for maximizing his own income—and impact on the world—Greenspan would be wasting his time. In a similar way, many companies waste their resources by putting their capital, their executives' years of education and experience, and long hours of work and dedication, at the service of unworthy corporate customers. That is, those who have no individual decision-making power, engage in group-think, pay little, are not loyal, and jump to another supplier at the first opportunity.

Why do companies serve such lousy customers? Out of inertia, because their people are used to the industry, because they have been taught that the customer is king, and because no one ever asked the revolutionary question: Why the heck are we serving these mopes? Why don't we fire them and find customers more worthy of our efforts? Why don't we leave this one-horse town where we only do laundry for miners, and go to the big city where our singing talents would be appreciated and where we could earn more?

When Munger became Buffett's partner, he convinced him that instead of buying and selling "three-puff cigar butts" frequently, he should look for cigars that "never run out"—companies that have strong "franchises." These are companies whose customers need them, cannot go to other suppliers, and are willing to pay for the privilege of being a customer. Such businesses are rare. But if you find one and sleuth it thoroughly, then buy it when its stock has temporarily crashed because of a transitory problem (which is also Seth Klarman's method, see Appendix A), and hold it for a long time. Not only would you make lots of money, but you would also postpone taxes. Furthermore, instead of buying and selling frequently, you'd be doing it rarely, and therefore have more time to enjoy your money and your family. In other words, you'd be piloting a plane that flies itself because it has a strong engine inside it that keeps taking it higher.

In your sleuthing efforts, you should keep in mind the two most important questions: Is this the kind of business I'd like to own indefinitely if I had to? Are this business's customers really worth serving? This does not mean you cannot occasionally sleuth for one-time wins, like mergers and acquisitions (as in the LBO example in Chapter 1) or for a two- to three-year winning streak or for the odd stock disaster going to zero, where you can double your money in a year. But the ideal (it's always good to keep one in mind) is to find the great company that you get to know intimately through sleuthing and that you can buy with confidence when it stumbles, like Coca-Cola, or American Express, or Gillette, or Geico.

And now we can get into the dynamics of sleuthing a company by getting to know the company's customers.

THE CUSTOMERS' KEY PEOPLE

Sleuthing a company's clients is similar to sleuthing the company's own employees and executives. However, a key difference is that there often are far more customers, so you must have a plan and an order of priorities so that your time isn't wasted.

If XYZ's customers are consumers, which could number in the millions, you'd have to choose a representative sample, and then check them out methodically according to the four criteria listed at the beginning of the chapter. But even if XYZ's customers are corporations, each will probably have as many people worth sleuthing as XYZ itself, so the total potential "sleuthees" would still be large. How do you decide who to investigate first and who last? If you have followed what has been said up to now closely, you must surely realize that your criteria need to be similar to those used by XYZ's VP of sales. In other words, you must focus on the customers who account for XYZ's highest revenues and highest growth potential. But once you do, you want to learn as much as you can about the specific *individuals* at the corporations who send XYZ checks. And, in addition, just to be on the safe side, you should also try to learn about the people at each corporation who have the power to recommend that checks be sent or to stop checks from being sent. Since check-sending is a sensitive function, it is usually divided into three separate activities performed by three different people. They are:

1. Those who recommend to send checks—product *users* and *vetters*

2. People with the power to decide that checks be sent—*decision makers*

3. Those who actually send the checks—*paymasters*

NEAR-IDEAL CUSTOMERS

From your point of view as an investor, the almost-ideal corporate customers are those where the product's users recommend it quickly, decision makers approve it fast, and purchasing officers pay for it soon after. At such a company, these three employee types work closely together in warm harmony to achieve the same goal, and are accessible by XYZ's salespeople directly, not via distributors.

Why is direct accessibility a requirement? If fast check-sending means XYZ does not have to waste time and money waiting for its revenue, then direct contact with the check senders means XYZ doesn't have to share these checks with any middlemen. In fact, sleuthing the customer follows closely the dictum of Deep Throat of Watergate fame—"Follow da money." Not theoretically, but physically. Who pays whom, for what, how, and when. This, indeed, is a key difference between stock analysts and sleuths: Stock analysts start their analysis with the company or its product. *Sleuths start with the customers*—da money and da money payers. This, after all, is why XYZ is in business—to get checks—and why you are considering its stock—to get their customer's money.

Soon you'll see an example of one near-ideal stock where Giraffe Capital, where I toil, made its customers three times their money in two years, using some simple customer sleuthing techniques that you, too, can use. But before we proceed, you may be asking: What about the *ideal* customers?

IDEAL CUSTOMERS

For these rare birds, three further conditions apply. First, and contrary to normal corporate practice, all three check-paying functions are performed by the same person. That is, the product user is also the decision maker and can also sign the checks. Second, as in the previous example, he or she is also directly reachable by XYZ's salesperson. But there's also a third condition. Not only does one person perform all these three functions, but beyond that—and this is extremely important—the product should fulfill not just the corporate needs, but the user's personal ones, too. This can be stated even more strongly: It is far more important that the product fulfill the *personal* needs of this ideal corporate buyer, than that it fulfill the buyer's *employer's* needs.

This is a subversive sort of rule, which is directly comparable to a secret agent addressing the personal needs of a competitor he is trying to recruit. Here, the salesperson sells a product that addresses the career and bonus needs of the *individual* check signer, *before* it addresses the corporate needs of the check signer's employer company. Is it fair to sell such products?

Before I answer that, let me tell you that the fastest-growing, most profitable products are often those where the buyer may even detract subtly from his employer's business value and hand it to the vendor. It is up to the employer's management to align their employees' interests with those of the corporation. If these aren't aligned, tough on the employer, because the employee will take care of his family's needs—as you would— before he sees to the needs of his employer's family.

This fact, though commonly known among salespeople, is not taught in business schools and certainly is not seen as a key reason for investing in a stock. This is just like facts commonly known only among intelligence operatives. For example, intelligence agents sometimes invest in the stock market for private gain, based on information they glean by physical sleuthing during their work. Similarly, when a corporate check writer finds buying or using the product *personally* advantageous, if he has the authority to buy, he will do so even if he thereby hands some of his employer's equity value to the vendor.

But back to the near-ideal, which in most cases is sure to make you rich over time. In this first example, I'll show you how to penetrate a company via its customers.

TALK TO CUSTOMERS BEFORE TALKING TO MANAGEMENT

One of the most common complaints about Wall Street and Bay Street analysts is that they are too close to company management, and so they merely parrot the company's line and puff the company's stocks, to later sell them to naïve investors. This may often be true, as several court documents regarding Internet stock underwriting reveal. Yet there's no denying that there's value in talking to management, if your intention is to find out what really goes on. Indeed, the entire first part of this book tried to teach you how to penetrate the company physically—be invited in—so as to get direct *sensory* information about what management is like—their personality, habits, motivation, and how they all work together. Brokerage analysts can do this easily, because they have the ear of money managers who run billions, so *their* phone calls to XYZ's management are returned, and if they want to come and visit, they are welcome.

But what about smaller investors like you? If you call XYZ's VP of sales or the CFO or the CEO, why would they even answer your call? It wouldn't make much sense for them to spend time on you—and, speaking frankly, they shouldn't. They have a company to run. For small investors like you, they have investor relations people to send you material and handle your queries. Furthermore, even if you are a bigger investor like Giraffe Capital, when a company is on the verge of landing a lucrative contract—precisely when we should be most interested and would want to see if management's eyes twinkle and hear if they whistle while they work—it is at that time especially that management will talk to no one, bigger investors included.

How to overcome this hurdle? First, remember that if management doesn't want to talk to you, it is not always negative. In fact, it may fuel my curiosity if management first evades me, because it shows that they are focused, or that they are busy with something big (either good or bad), or that they are buying stock themselves and don't want anyone driving up its price by buying it too. Keep in mind that the opposite can also be true. When management is overly eager to promote their stock, I often cool right off. The less promotional they are, the more interested I am, and so should you be.

But what if management avoids you and you still want to talk to them? How can you get them to call you back? As shown before, one way is to meet them at the annual meeting, or elsewhere, then use cold reading of individual managers to establish warm personal relations, and do to them what XYZ's Sales VP does to his customers: Get close to them and get them to accept you as trustworthy. But what if you can't do this very well, and you still want XYZ's management to return your calls? How can you get them to do that? Very simply: You must insert yourself between XYZ and its customers in such a way that they *have* to talk to you.

POWER FLOWS FROM THE CUSTOMERS' DOLLARS

Customers are a company's lifeblood, and customer relationships are the veins through which the corporate lifeblood—dollars—flows. Therefore, anyone with a thumb on this vein has power, money, and plenty of attention. It can be an outside distributor who can direct business to various suppliers, a legislator on a key committee looking for a political contribution from XYZ, the receiving clerk who assigns parking slots to XYZ's trucks, or most often XYZ's top salespeople, who receive bonuses for their customers' connections. Indeed, that's why the top salespeople of any company get so much attention from the company's top brass. And that's why if you want a company's top brass to pay attention to you as well, you must befriend their customers like a *salesperson* and learn things XYZ's own people don't know.

This is not rocket science. It's simply Politics 101. Place your finger on the corporate bloodline and press lightly, and the XYZ folks will snap to attention and talk to you. That's what foreign governments do when they form close contacts with leading politicians at the largest oil-producing province in an otherwise oil-poor country, in order to get leverage with that country's central government. That's what intelligence agents do when they form close contacts with important members of the opposing organization on a human, personal level. That's what police detectives do when they befriend family members of key distributors of illicit merchandise whose producers' organization they want to penetrate. And that's what you should do too. Get between XYZ and its customers' check senders, and you'll get management's attention.

And now for the inevitable warnings and caveats. Be extraordinarily careful you do not hurt XYZ by doing this. And whatever you learn, be it professional or personal information, *keep it absolutely confidential.* If at all possible, do not take notes. If you do, keep them secure. And certainly do not tell the customers titillating tales about XYZ's personnel, especially if you have already penetrated XYZ's headquarters. Similarly, do not tell

XYZ people any tales about their customers, unless these are unresolved issues that, if resolved, would benefit both company and customers. And even then, try to do this in a way that hides the identity of specific informants—again as an intelligence operative would, denying the opposition knowledge of his specific sources.

If you act this way, honorably and discreetly, providing benefits both to XYZ and to your sources among its customers, then even if at first XYZ may have been wary of you, eventually its people will treat you as a trusted, helpful shareholder, and then you will *really* get to penetrate the company's business. Now for the obvious question: What about the legality of all this?

INSIDE AND OUTSIDE INFORMATION

The general rule is: Information you get from a company's customers is, in most cases, not inside information. It is *outside* information. This is the type of knowledge that eventually creates information about what is happening inside. If you learn of customers' intentions directly from them, you'll often end up knowing about sales even *before* XYZ does. This is the kind of information that stock analysts should be trying very hard to get, but few do because most analysts do not want to annoy XYZ's management. Furthermore, analysts often won't try to analyze companies that generate cash and do not need to sell stock, as you'll see in the example below. Thus, seeking information from a company's customers, although obviously a no-brainer, is often a wide-open field that you can exploit.

THE FIELD IS WIDE OPEN

You may now be asking, what about professional fund managers who control hundreds of millions or billions of dollars? Don't they call customers of companies in whose stocks they invest? The sad fact is that very few do. Any one of those big fund managers has 80 to 100 stocks in his or her portfolio, and often more. Surely you can't expect them to do as much work as that! But, you might still insist, what about hedge funds? These are run by smart cookies who are deeply experienced in the market. Surely they call companies' clients, suppliers, and people, and sleuth for *physical* evidence of coming sales or disasters? The answer is that very few, if any, do. (More about how I know this in the next section.)

Please remember that most investors, including the most sophisticated—*especially* the most sophisticated—think of stocks as mere symbols and data, and invest in them based only on second- and thirdhand information, which they then manipulate by spreadsheets and computer models and logic and theory. These investors are similar to those intelligence agencies that pore over satellite pictures and perform mathematical analysis of radio intercepts in their clean, air-conditioned office. Sleuths are more like the agents who go out into the hot dirty field, dressed in a native gallabiah to chat with the opponents in their Faluja barbershops in their local idiom and learn what they're really up to.

If you still don't believe that most hedge funds invest solely based on secondhand symbolic information, there's good, though inadvertent, evidence of this in a recent delightful book about hedge funds, *Hedgehogging*, by Barton Biggs, which I highly recommend and which you should find constructive.

Barton Biggs, who once ran the research department at Morgan Stanley and oversaw the firm's stock analysts, later became the firm's global strategist, producing weekly, wonderfully readable investment "think pieces" based primarily on symbolic information. (This means he did not stake out LBO firms' offices or count the number of trucks shipping product, but probably used secondhand print and screen information as input for his opinions.) After his long and illustrious career at Morgan Stanley, Biggs resigned and went off to start a hedge fund with a few partners and then to write about his adventure.

In his book, Biggs reports that thousands of new hedge funds are started every year and that the majority of the "hedgies" who run them, once they have raised their money, stay in their offices, where they gaze at their Bloomberg terminals all day for investment ideas. In other words, all these money managers see the same secondhand data that everyone else sees. They also talk by phone with the same analysts, to get the same earnings estimates that everyone else gets—through Turing's wall slot, as it were. Thus, the hidden, implicit assumption by all these hedgies is that the secondhand symbolic information already known to all, is sufficient to help *them* outdo all *others* since *they* have better brains.

But are better brains indeed sufficient? In some rare cases they might be. There are, after all, some rare genius investors who can sit in their offices, read nothing but ValueLine one-page reports, and do very well over time. Buffett, Munger, Gross, Kahn—these are investment grandmasters who can play chess against the entire world on an open chessboard and win.

I am not a genius, yet my money management firm does well. For those of us who are a little shy of grandmaster genius level, physical sleuthing can provide the edge. How many geniuses are there among these hedge fund runners who use secondhand, screen- and print-based information only? Apparently very few. As Barton Biggs wryly reports, of the thousands of hedge funds started every year, the majority close down. It seems that brains alone are not sufficient for investment success, if they are fed solely with secondhand symbols.

Biggs also covers other kinds of hedgies, called *quants*, who, in a far closer approximation of a Turing Test, forgo *any* nonnumerical information and just crunch numbers in order to find patterns that forecast stock price movements; this is strictly based on secondhand data. How well do these quant funds do? On average, not much better. Therefore, the obvious question anyone should now be asking is: Is it possible that the edge in investing is not in manipulating data better, but in getting *exclusive* data? On this Barton Biggs says nothing. In fact, his book seems oblivious to the question as are the hedgies he quotes. Odd as it may sound, not once in the entire book could I find an example of a hedge fund manager who goes out to sleuth for *physical, exclusive* information. This brings me to the second, instructive part of *Hedgehogging*, where Barton Biggs tells how his firm decided to short oil.

LARGE BETS ON CARDS EVERYONE CAN SEE

When oil was climbing, Barton's partners reached the conclusion that its price was too high, and the best course for making money was to sell it short. Did they know something others did not? No, they didn't. Did they have any exclusive *physical* info, such as private scouts in Saudi

Arabia who knew of secret new wells about to come into production, so as to expand the world oil supply beyond the commonly expected? Not at all. Did they perhaps hear of an undisclosed government decision to release oil from the strategic reserve, so as to increase supply unexpectedly? Not that either. Did they have *any* other exclusive information not available to others, based on which they were ready to risk millions of clients' money in the market? Again, no.

By taking a short position based on secondhand data, Biggs's crew apparently acted on the implicit assumption that all modern investment boffins make—that Turing's question can be answered in the affirmative. Yes, superior brains poring over symbolic representations of the world *can* beat all *other* brains that see the same symbols, through sheer manipulative power.

How valid is this assumption? Apparently not at all, since most newly opened hedge funds operating on these hidden assumptions close. Yet that doesn't faze new fund runners. Surely, they must be saying, *our* brains are better. And so they join the index fund investors and shove their money through Turing's wall slot.

How did Biggs's oil short work out? After a long period of time, the investment ultimately went their way, but the firm risked a lot of money to achieve a total return that was just about equal to that of some long-term value investing strategies. Brains, at least in this case, were not enough. And yet the objective of identifying hidden value strictly by symbols lingers. If being very brainy is not enough to make money in stocks using symbolic data, perhaps the answer is to be super-brainy? Perhaps Turing's question can be answered in the affirmative but just not by everyone? Perhaps if you use computers to help your reasoning power, you can take the money of those who don't? Maybe, just maybe, Turing's question can be answered affirmatively only by a very, very few super-clever questioners—whose fancy forecasting methods, once learned, could help you make money by merely gazing at the screen in the comfort of your air-conditioned office? The demise of Long Term Capital (LTC), a giant hedge fund that employed several Nobel winners specializing in EMT, seems to refute this assumption also.

To be fair, many quants combine fundamental data that include financial and accounting figures together with price and other market information (for example, sales and purchases of stock by insiders). But still, they forecast stock prices based on symbols, making the implicit assumption that the individual and specific human dramas of commerce can be generalized via math and letters. Some quants even manage to make money for a while—just as some insurance companies manage to make money for a while by writing hurricane insurance cheaply. But when a hurricane arrives, the money made is often seen not as money gained but money borrowed.

And now for some commercial drama—here is the story of the long-promised near-ideal company.

SMALLTECH INC.: UNIQUE NICHE, CHEAP STOCK

Smalltech (a fictitious company) was a public software company that provided management software to small towns, municipalities, and town-owned utilities to help keep track of tax payments, employees, budgets, and the like. The check payers were mainly town managers, municipal accountants, and utilities' CFOs, most of whom had the authority to make the purchase decision. These check payers also used the software themselves, alongside their small teams. Total revenues of Smalltech were less than $100 million, down 33 percent from the peak.

Why the decline? A botched takeover attempt, foolish lawsuits against customers, hapless boardroom bickering—in a word, inadequate management. And yet, throughout its travails, in its narrow niche Smalltech kept a 30 percent market share, whereas the nearest competitor had only 10 percent. And since the niche was too small for the software biggies like SAP, Baan, and Oracle, Smalltech's business was quite secure.

How did we find the stock? It came up both through our extensive databases and from discussions over beer (a useful research tool) with various executives in the software business whom we asked, "Which company would you have liked to own for your family forever?"

Now, when executives said "Smalltech," they really meant they would love to own it *if they could also run it*, because it was clear that the company had outgrown its original entrepreneurial founders and needed professional management. What was also clear, aside from bad manage-

ment and a so-so-board, was that Smalltech was terrific. Its employees
were good, its market niche secure, and its customers loyal and depend-
ent on the product. Last but not least, by all criteria of value, the stock
was extremely cheap. Then again, the company was losing money.

LOSSES BEING STEMMED

Then one evening, in a standard weekly computer-run, I noticed that
losses were declining and the trend was inching toward profit. At the
same time, a text search brought up the company's name as one where a
new CEO had just been hired. (You can have a text search run on the
Bloomberg machine, as a useful sleuthing aid. Or you can run a similar
one simply on Google or Yahoo. You can search for all appointments of
new management, all dismissals of marketing VPs, or all takeover offers,
etc.) So here was a company with a unique business and cheap stock, and
now it also had new management, that was apparently instituting enough
changes to start stemming the losses. My ears perked up, because if the
company could regain profitability, the stock price was clearly a bargain.

ATTEMPT TO CONTACT
MANAGEMENT UNSUCCESSFUL

But could the company regain profitability? I placed a call to the new
CEO and was shunted to his voice mail. I left a message, telling him I was
a money manager interested in the stock, but the CEO never called back.
A second message still got no response. I called the CFO. Ditto. I got
nada. Yet I wasn't at all angry. Smalltech's new management had a tough
job to do—turning around the business—and I was not part of it. They
were focused. Yet I wanted to learn what went on. So what did I do next?

As you probably guessed, I decided to insert myself between the company and its clients—the three types of individuals who sent them
checks. Years ago, finding these people was a lengthy process that
involved calling customer-companies, tracking names of product users,
accounting personnel, obtaining references, and calling them until you
got what you were after. This was doable, but tedious.

But today we have the Internet. You see, Smalltech had what is called a
users group. Most smart companies organize such groups, where clients tell

them what they like about its products, and what they want to see improved. Companies that follow such feedback usually do best. Smalltech had several users groups, which was in itself a sign of a good company. They had one group for each market segment, each headed by a coordinator. The names, phone numbers, and e-mail addresses of the coordinators were provided on Smalltech's website. I cleared my desk and my calendar, and then my assistant and I began to make calls.

MARCHING ORDERS TO SELF

In Chapter 1 I gave you the analogy of an intelligence service getting its marching orders from the general who seeks answers to specific questions. In Smalltech's case, the objectives I gave myself and my research assistant were the following:

First, get the answers to the four questions listed at the beginning of the chapter.

Second, find the three types of check senders.

Third, find answers to the following:

Is the new CEO's plan working?

Are clients buying into it?

How likely is Smalltech to turn a profit?

When you start sleuthing, you would do well to keep a similar list of main questions before you. Of course, as you get deeper into the method, don't be surprised if you realize that other questions, which you hadn't previously thought of, become more important.

CALLING A COMPANY'S CLIENTS

It took me several weeks to chat with 17 Smalltech clients, both in the United States and in Canada. Later, I met a few personally to gather physical evidence of the product's use and about those who use it—where they sit, what they do, and whom they interact with. At that time I still had not spoken to management, although they were probably very aware by then that a Canadian money manager was checking them out. The silence was unusual. In three out of four cases, I would have received a call from the company before my inquiries were over, asking what the heck my interest was. At the very least, management would want to make sure I was not checking them out in order to take them over—a high probability for a company whose stock is cheap. Once you start sleuthing a company's customers, you too may get a call from the company asking why you are interested. (This is what you might want.) Yet I didn't, probably because Smalltech's new management was truly focused on the turnaround. I liked that.

WHAT TO ASK THE COMPANY'S CLIENTS

You might wonder what I told Smalltech's customers when they picked up the phone. I introduced myself and simply said that I was a money manager and an investor doing research about a company whose product they were using, and that their input was important. I said I was running a pension fund (which was true), leaving the image of widows and orphans to hover in the background. I waited for Smalltech's customers to ask me how they could help—once they did, the job was half done. But even if they didn't ask, I inquired whether or not they minded helping me out.

What did I ask Smalltech's customers? First and foremost, I asked them to tell me about their jobs, how Smalltech's software fit into their work, and how it helped them do it better. Then I shut up and let them talk. And did they ever! In general, working people are eager to talk about their jobs, which in many cases are a big part of their lives, yet few around them are willing to listen. If you are sincere—and I am—they will open up to you.

So I asked, and they talked. Once they began, I occasionally asked clarifying questions: how they came to do this job, who they worked closely with in the company, how they came to hear about the product, whether others in the company used it also, and what were their names? And would they mind if I talked to them too? What about friends in other companies, towns, or utilities who used it? I took down all these names and then asked—delicately—who had made the decision to buy the product, who paid for it, and how. Was it a one-time payment? These payments often take a long time to make because they go off capital expenditures, which are depreciated and have corporate impact. Or were they pay-as-you-go? These are expensed and can be made by divisional managers. I asked how long the purchase decision took. Did they consider other products? Which ones? And if so, *why did they buy this one?*

Let me stop here and flag the last question because this is key. Asking this question right off the bat is a mistake in my opinion—often a grave mistake. Very few check senders would admit that they bought a product because it gave them a personal advantage. They would certainly not admit this if this personal advantage came at the slight, or more than slight, expense of their employer. (It wasn't the case here.) But once you get the user talking, after establishing trust—yes, even over the phone it can be done—you can get close to the real reason the product was bought, which is what you are really after.

Try to arrange a personal meeting if you are not comfortable chatting over the phone. If this doesn't work for you either, ask a smart family member to do this for you or ask a member of your investment club, a friend, even an assistant or a junior worker. The ability to get answers to questions and follow where they lead is not natural to everyone, but it is also not necessarily correlated with education or super-brains. It is a human skill that can be learned. I suggest you try to do it yourself, because the more you do it, the better you'll become.

EVERY COMPANY IS A HUMAN DRAMA

Once you can answer the four crucial questions, you'll likely understand a company's business. But you'll also probably get a sense of the individual drama within the company—which no formula or printed page can generalize—via the gossip you'll hear about the company's background, its people and their foibles, and any other scuttlebutt. When I spoke with Smalltech's clients I learned how the company sank into trouble, how the original entrepreneurs got into a tiff with the board and sold their shares to a competitor who then unsuccessfully tried to take Smalltech over, how the board reacted, the lawsuits that ensued, the upheaval that caused the company to lose focus, and how the new CEO was trying to clean all of this up.

It was a veritable soap opera—as many cheap stocks often are—and the kind of story analysts never tell you, but which gives you a real insight into why a company has fallen into trouble and why it might be coming out of it. And I got all of it by merely listening to Smalltech's clients. I got names and descriptions of the main executives, managers, and key employees, their relationships and their conflicts and their alliances. It seemed like the usual dysfunction of a company after a rough patch. Yet when I asked how many customers Smalltech had lost throughout its troubles, I learned that nearly all customers remained with the company through the ordeal. Why did they stay? Because, as more than one customer said, the product was so good and so unique and so indispensable to their operations that they didn't really have any choice. (This came as close as I ever heard to Charlie Munger's definition of a "franchise.")

I asked for the customers' opinion of the new CEO's plan, and most had a very clear concept of it—both because the product was so important to them that they took the trouble to learn about it, and because the new CEO had visited all key customers and relayed it to them in person. Almost all approved of the plan; the only ones who were lukewarm were marginal clients whom the CEO intended to cut off for a variety of business reasons. I learned all this and more. Indeed, the rapport I developed with Smalltech's customers was so close that when a Smalltech executive in charge of customer relations who had left to join a minor competitor returned, I heard the customers' raves about it within a day.

There was one more event of note.

INSIDERS BUYING

About that time there appeared a relentless, ongoing wave of stock buying by Smalltech insiders: managers, directors, vice presidents, all of whom must file reports about it with the SEC, which publishes the information. But I also learned from their customers that lower-level employees were buying, too. This told me that not only did the customers have confidence in the company's future, but so did former executives who rejoined the firm as well as company insiders who bought stock in the market with their after-tax dollars.

For most money managers, this would be enough to make them buy some stock. But money sleuths do not buy a little stock. We buy a lot. And for this we must be sure of our facts and especially of the human element. So now, at long last, when I knew nearly as much as Smalltech's executives did about the business, the time had come to speak with the management.

I called the CEO and left a message with the assistant who answered the CEO's phone.

A CALL TO THE CEO

I introduced myself as a fund manager interested in the company, and told the assistant that I had talked to several individual customers at the A, B, and C organizations. All customers gave the company—and the CEO in particular—high marks, but a few noted there were minor product shortcomings that a competitor was about to exploit. I mentioned the competitor and the product in question. Could the CEO please call me so I could ask him about these? I thanked the assistant, hung up, and waited. The CEO called back within the hour, and we had a pleasant half-hour chat. You might wonder what I asked the CEO.

First, I gave him my feedback from clients, letting him know of the attempt by competitors to exploit the minor shortcoming. One competitor he apparently did know about, the others he didn't. When he thanked me, I asked about his plan. I made it clear that I was asking for no forecasts, no information that had not been made public, just his personal take on the plan to make the company profitable and return it to growth. And I started by asking about his own background and experience. Then I stopped speaking and listened.

Of course, he talked. First, because he owed me one for informing him about a competitor's move, and if there's one strong sense common to all business people it is one of reciprocity. You do me a favor, I'll do you one. But second, when you ask a person to talk about himself, few can resist. So here I had two forces acting in my favor. While he spoke, I occasionally asked about people he had brought along with him, their expertise, and the challenges as he saw them. I tried to read the CEO over the phone so as to style my questions properly. I complimented him honestly on real achievements to date. I asked about shortcomings in the plan. Finally I asked whether I could speak to his chief financial officer. The CEO agreed and told me to call her. I did, and got as good an impression of her as I had gotten of the CEO. Was it time to buy? Almost, but not quite.

THOROUGH CHECKING OF THE PRODUCT

Before buying stock, I had to make sure the product was indeed as good as users thought it was, and would not become obsolete in a year. So I commissioned a software engineer to evaluate the product. It cost me two thousand bucks, which isn't cheap, but it is a small cost when compared to the profit potential. Is this something that you should be doing? Perhaps not at the beginning. But you could try to find a techie who understands what the experts mean, and then will speak with the experts on your behalf. Or you can find names of experts over the Internet. Some might even give you their opinion for free, if you are polite. Try it—you'd be surprised what initiative and persistence will get you. Some may charge a small amount and if the question is critical to your decision, it may be worth it.

And what if you don't like technology, or don't understand it? No problem. You don't have to invest in tech companies. You can invest in low tech or in no tech. There are plenty of niches to choose from; choose the one you understand. Warren Buffett, to take but one example, doesn't understand technology, so he invests in other areas.

Back to Smalltech. The engineer took one week to evaluate the product. His conclusion was that it was stable and served its purpose well, even though it was not Windows-based. What of the competition? I asked the engineer to check with salespeople at the big software shops—Oracle, Baan, SAP—all with revenues in the billions—and ask if they would bid on a fictional contract by some unspecified small town.

In intelligence circles this is called "false flag recruiting." Is it ethical? Not if I was damaging those I called, and here I didn't. Besides, I was trying to find out whether I should entrust my family's money and my clients' families' money to strangers. At any rate, all salesmen my engineer friend called laughed out loud. Bid on a software contract for a small town? You must be joking! It would be too small for Biggies like us! One of the salespeople even said outright, "Call Smalltech." I was now sure Smalltech was safe from the hard competition. I also knew its new management was doing a fine job. Its customers loved the product. Losses were being stemmed. The product was good. The stock was cheap.

So now came the final, obvious question: If everything was so upbeat, why were so many brokers' analysts ignoring the stock?

BROKERS' ANALYSTS WORK FOR THEIR KIDS, NOT YOURS

I called two analysts who had followed the stock when it was at $20 (it was now at $1.50), and asked them directly. I learned there were two obvious reasons—those I should have known myself. First, Smalltech's stock was so cheap that its market capitalization was small. Therefore, it wasn't trading in enough volume to justify following, since any commission on the trading would be negligible. But second, and most important, Smalltech had cash on hand and was now beginning to generate more. It would therefore have no need to sell any new treasury stock, which is what brokers are really in business for. Why then would any sane broker follow Smalltech's stock or recommend it? Brokers want to promote stocks whose companies need cash or, as a second priority, to trade their stocks in volume. *Often the best stocks to buy are those that brokers neglect.*

Most investors see a broker's neglect as a negative because they can't get research on a company and so have to do research themselves. For sleuths, a broker's disregard is often a blessing. It means that if you find a gem, no one else may know how good it is, so there is no competition for the shares. Smalltech fitted neither moneymaking category for brokers, so they ignored it. Therefore, when we began to buy the stock in the market for our clients, we had no competition except by the company's executives, who were still buying, so we had no difficulty establishing a good position.

How long did it take, from first noticing Smalltech until the first stock purchase? About three months. Was all this time spent sleuthing one company? No. At the time, Smalltech was one of three companies we sleuthed. (We bought one of the other two, dropping the second after its flaws became obvious.) Instead of learning only a little about many mediocre stocks and buying all to diversify, stock sleuths prefer to know nearly everything about a very few superb stocks, because it gives them such confidence in the stock's future that they can take a meaningful position, and stay with it even as the stock fluctuates.

We put a fair portion of our clients' money into Smalltech, and as the company broke into profit and its stock climbed—only a little, yes, because still no broker followed it—we kept buying for the existing clients and for new clients that came in. Two years later, after seeing its profits soar and declaring a dividend, and resisting a creeping takeover by one large shareholder, the company was taken over by a discerning corporate buyer at three times our initial cost. A triple in two and a half years.

LESSONS LEARNED FROM SLEUTHING SMALLTECH

Let's pause and see what you can learn from this example.

1. When you sleuth a company, check first to see if they have user groups and, if so, who are the contact persons or coordinators. Calling them can save you a lot of time and give you a quick understanding of the business *from the customer's point of view*, which, of course, is what you are after.

2. Your own *personal* contact with a company's customers is essential and should play a major role in all your investment decisions. Call them. Get out of the house or office and meet them. For this reason, you should make it a rule to *never, ever invest in the stock of any company until you have talked to at least three of its key customers.* If you follow this dictum alone, it will save you more money than most other investment activities.

3. When you talk to customers, ask them first about *their* jobs. This is more than a ruse to gain their trust. First, it will tell you whether the customer is a user, an approver, or a paymaster. Second, it will show you how the product fits into the customer's job, and whether it satisfies only corporate needs or personal ones, too. But third, it will show you if the customer is worth serving at all. Just as some products are not worth making, so are some customers not worth serving. And when sleuthing a company, don't start with the product. Start with the customer.

4. Inquire about the sales cycle. How did the product come to the customer's attention? How long was it before it was bought? Who approved it? Who resisted it, if anyone? What follow-up was performed by the vendor?

5. Last, but by no means least, ask about the customer's impression of the vendor's people, and about any ancillary information he or she can provide. This usually leads to gossip. Listen carefully to what you hear! Many such tales can prove important, especially if they indicate that the vendor has problems that are not publicly known, problems like the escapades of Company A's president in the research project for my MBA class, as described in the Introduction. But, as noted before, keep such information to yourself and do nothing that may cause strife between the company and its clients—ever. Act with honor, and you shall be repaid.

NEAR PERFECT VERSUS PERFECT

I consider Smalltech only a *near*-ideal investment because of three slight imperfections. First, the company's customers—the towns' and small utilities' accounting personnel—had to get the manager's approval and the financial officer's signature on the check. But since both the CFO and CAO also used the software, and there really was no significant alternative product, the process was fast and smooth. Second, approval did require meetings, so the sales process lasted a few months. And—the third deficiency—the benefit for the buyer or decision maker was not personal, such as a bonus, but an organizational benefit. However, the users earned strong career brownie points, which in several cases led to promotions and gave some town mayors a strong leg-up on re-election. But other than these three shortcomings, Smalltech was as near perfect an investment as I could wish for.

Yet there is one characteristic that, if found in a product, can really make a company a perfect investment—if the product gives the buyer a personal advantage. If the individual user or check signer is in an intensely competitive business and the product gives him or her a personal advantage against competitors, then the product will fly off the shelves.

If all these conditions apply, then the company's sales will skyrocket, its stock will zoom, and its shareholders will make a fortune. The example below details a company that I consider to be one of the most perfect tech companies I've ever seen, where the gain was more than 20 times the original investment in three years. Of course, we never made all this gain—no one buys at the exact bottom, and furthermore, we deem it prudent to start selling once we have a certain large profit and the stock is no longer cheap. But we made more than enough to have fond memories of the company.

ALPACA SYSTEMS

The product sold by Alpaca Systems (a fictitious company located in Canada) was based on the same principle as sleuthing—that all business flows from customers. The premise of the Alpaca Systems software was that if salespeople have the customer's *personal* information in front of their eyes when they talk to him or her, the salesperson can make the customer feel cherished and loved like a dear friend, and thereby benefit from extra sales. That software is called a customer relationship management (CRM) system. Alpaca was neither the first nor the only CRM company around at the time, and, in fact, Laird (also fictitious) was the largest player among a field of several others of respectable sizes. Alpaca decided to differentiate itself by focusing on a niche market—in software this is termed "vertical"—serving medium-size retail stockbrokers, which was a market too small for Laird. This niche strategy was similar to Smalltech's, which is what drew me to Alpaca's stock. So I began to sleuth around to find more about it.

THE SLEUTHING BEGINS

I found that Alpaca's managers were top-notch in all four key areas: general management, marketing, finance, and R&D. And the product was a dilly. When a broker's client called, a screen popped up that showed the client's portfolio, a summary of his or her past calls, stocks bought and sold, and any past instructions regarding future buy or sell intentions. It also detailed the client's family situation, hobbies, strong likes and dislikes, eccentricities and foibles, club memberships, golf score, if any, corporate affiliations, board memberships if any, address, photographs, and any other personal details the broker thought important enough to include.

This list was, in essence, a scaled-down version of an intelligence service's database of "persons of interest." Both the police and intelligence services keep similar, but larger and more elaborate, databases. For example, when an agent snaps a picture of an opponent's operative in Jakarta, the database can immediately bring up all the past associations and affiliations of that person. The Mossad, for instance, is rumored to have a most detailed computer system called Kshareem ("Connections," in Hebrew), which agents can tap into. (In Chapter 6 we'll see how you can use this principle when putting all sleuthing data into one display, called a *Starmap*.)

Who kept Alpaca's database up-to-date? Some data was keyed in by the broker, and the rest by the broker's assistant, based on the broker's notes. The program, of course, did what any stock sleuth tries to do before he or she befriends an informant—keep his background in mind so as to direct the conversation and make it personal. Here's how the software works.

Say you are a broker and a customer calls you. As you pick up the phone, a screen pops up with the client's portfolio and recent requests. At the same time, it reminds you that this customer lost money in oil stocks, so please be careful talking to him about oil. However, he is proud of selling his tech stocks at the peak, as well as of his golf game, especially the time he beat you. So you can occasionally compliment him on both. Furthermore, his birthday was yesterday, for which his wife was supposed to take him to a French restaurant (which you noted), and he was supposed to pick the wine. Also, last time you and he talked, he had mentioned his coming fly-fishing trip, his inner debate about the wine choice, and about transferring his large retirement account from his current investment bank to your firm.

After you wish him a happy birthday, inquire about his wine choice and about the size of the fish he caught, and ask him deferentially about his opinion about the tech market; do you think you can also convince him to transfer his account to your firm? If you cannot, you don't belong in the brokerage business.

Back to Alpaca. Alpaca was a public company for about two years when I heard about its product from some broker friends. I realized that the principle behind it was genius, and because the narrow market niche reminded me of Smalltech and the stock was cheap (a key requirement for me), I decided to check the company out further. I visited a few retail brokers who used the software and found that it seemed to work well. Alpaca's management was good, the stock was cheap, and I was tempted to buy it. But caution prevailed, and I decided to look deeper into the process of how it was sold. Who exactly decided to buy it? Who approved it?

DEEPER SLEUTHING UNEARTHS DEEP FLAWS

I took a few retail brokers to lunch and sought answers to the four key questions. It was lucky I did, because while seeking these answers, I found some otherwise hidden flaws that cooled my interest. The following should prove to you (if you still need proof) that there's no substitute for speaking directly with customers of a company whose stock you are considering, to understand the customers' *personal* motivation and needs.

I found that the software product was sold to retail brokerage firms for use by the brokers, who, especially at the midsize firms, are the lowest folks on the totem pole and must accept whatever software the firm supplies. The software was distributed on disk via computer retail stores and sold to the retail brokers' manager, a sort of whip-master whose job it is to exhort the brokers to push the customers to trade more and to flog more of the firm's underwriting.

What no analyst would tell you, however (and what I learned during my many meetings with retail brokers over beer), is that another, unspoken job of the manager/whip-master is to ensure that if a disgruntled broker decamps to another firm, his or her clients stay behind. From his or her perspective, the clients belong to the firm, not to the individual brokers. Do the brokers have the same view? No way. Retail brokers see their clients as theirs, and so guard their clients' data zealously, often keeping daily copies at home, so that if the whip-master's exhortations become too stringent, or the firm's underwritings too crappy, the broker can take his or her clients and leave for another firm. When I finally understood this, it dawned on me that Alpaca's product was being sold to the *wrong customers*. The real customer—the user—was the broker, not his or her manager. To make this clear, let's analyze the needs of both. According to the three check-sending functions:

1. Who is the decision maker? The retail brokers' manager

2. Who would use the product? The retail brokers

3. Who would send the checks? The brokerage's firm CFO

Based on this information, I could now predict fairly accurately that the product would not be used, in its present form, nor would users recommend it to other brokers. To see this more clearly, look at the answers to the four questions for the obvious conflict:

1. **WHO WERE THE CUSTOMERS?** The retail brokers' manager *and* the retail brokers were the customers.

2. **WHAT EXACTLY WAS EACH BUYING?** The manager was *buying control* of the brokers. The brokers were getting *help in production* but were *paying with loss of control* over their clients, which reduced their equity in the assets on "their" books.

3. **WHAT EXACTLY WAS ALPACA SELLING?** It thought it was selling productivity but what it *also* sold was control over brokers, without even realizing it.

4. **WHY WOULD THE BROKERS' MANAGER BUY IT?** Managers would buy the software because they saw the product advertised, because the computer store's owner showed it to them, because the managers' bonuses would rise if their brokers produced more, but also because managers gave their own bosses—the chairman and the president, who were the brokerage firm's shareholders—more control over the *brokers' clients.*

Indeed, those who benefited the most were the brokerage firm's shareholders—like absentee lords on whose lands sheep herders brought sheep to graze. If the land overseers became too harsh and herders wanted to leave with their sheep, the lord would say, "You can go, but the sheep are mine." Alpaca's initial software was aimed both at helping fleece the sheep more thoroughly and at making sure they became the property of the lord, not his herders.

But what of the herders—the brokers? Why would they use the software? Yes, it helped them shear the sheep more closely by feigning friendliness. And it was convenient to use, because the overseer/manager had installed it on their computers. But would they really use it?

I found it no surprise that brokers kept their old records, maintained copies at home, and even worse that they actively sabotaged the new software. Why the active sabotage? As I wined and dined more brokers—Alpaca's end-customers—I realized that commission income was only one source of their wealth. Switching firms or having their firm bought out was another. Because when retail brokers decided to switch firms (for a higher split of the commission, for access to better and more honest research, or for more accommodating and humane supervision), if they could bring their clients along to the new firm, that firm would pay them about one year's annual commission as a bonus. Similarly, if the broker's old firm was acquired by another firm, the remaining brokers would get about one year's commission as a retaining bonus—for fear they would decamp with their clients to another firm.

Once I learned this, I understood that Alpaca's product was a dud. While Alpaca thought it was only selling higher productivity to its product's users, it was also unknowingly helping its users' employers enslave them. This is one of the best examples I can give you of a strategic mistake. And it is one I would likely never have grasped if I had not talked to the final product users directly. Certainly no brokerage analyst would dare write up the above in a research report.

Alpaca's mistake was fatal. By selling its splendid product to the wrong customers, it nearly went broke. Luckily, due to my chats with its real customers, I did not buy the stock and avoided losing money. (This is further proof, if you still needed one, that the "Don't Buy" decision as a benefit of sleuthing is often as important as the "Buy.")

ALPACA FINDS ITS REAL CUSTOMERS

I withdrew my attention, leaving the stock on my database for an occasional look-see. And it was lucky I did, because then something happened that made me sit up and take notice of Alpaca all over again. Alpaca, in effect, fired its clients and got itself new ones. To state it more precisely, Alpaca stopped selling its software to its clients' bosses via computer stores, and began to sell to its true clients—the stockbrokers—directly.

I learned this by accident from some stockbrokers I had befriended during my first sleuthing expedition (and who were now calling me to try to get me to move my account). I learned that not only did Alpaca stop selling to its clients' competition, but it also narrowed its focus and now sold only to the highest-earning brokers on the Street. And what it now sold these brokers was exactly what they had wanted—a tool both to help them earn more commission money and to gain more control over "their" clients. So if a broker moved, it was more likely "his" or "her" clients would move also. Yes, it would come at the expense of the employer, in that the product would help the brokers make higher commission and also peel away some value from their employer's equity and put it into their own pockets.

Was it ethical? I think so. Neither the firm nor the stockbrokers were more entitled than the other to the benefit of selling the clients, so there is not much moral difference between helping a company control its brokers' clients and helping the brokers keep control over them. Both are commercial interests, standing in opposition to each other, and so long as you do not break the law and make no false promises, you can choose any side as your customers, as Alpaca did. Only this time it chose the right ones—the brokers themselves. The implied sales pitch was simple, though couched in polite euphemisms, which I will hereby translate for you. The implied pitch went as follows:

"You, high-level broker Joe Q., are making $200,000 a year in commission income. We'll help you make $300,000 by making each client think you are his or her bosom buddy. But not just that, we'll also help you tie the clients strongly to you, not your firm, by having all their data on your computer on a disk which—incidentally—can be taken home prudently for safekeeping. So that if you move to another firm, you can be paid an additional $300,000 in return for *your* clients, who will now surely go with you. The cost to you? Say $5,000 a year in software license fees. You want?"

OVERWHELMING RESPONSE

The response was overwhelming, and Alpaca experienced growth of nearly 100 percent per year. Indeed, once stockbrokers began to talk among themselves about the new software, Alpaca began to get phone calls from as far away as Italy. Why the explosive interest? Because the product now addressed the *personal* need of the best kind of client *directly*. The client was best because he or she was the decision maker, vetter, and payer *all in one*. The benefit was to him or her personally, and the cost to him or her was low in relation to the personal benefit. In addition, the brokerage business is intensely competitive, so that if one broker buys the Alpaca software and it works, those who don't buy it may lose out over time. Therefore, the buy decision was near instantaneous, even though it went against the interests of the employer.

The two key points you should take away from this discussion are:

- It is critical to see the product or service you are sleuthing as fulfilling the needs of the *individuals* who use it, vet it, and send checks—*even if this benefit comes at the expense of their employer.*

- There's no substitute for *personal* conversations with users because these often unearth information that no one puts in writing. Certainly no research analyst dared say what I had said above, either in print or orally.

Once Alpaca's new clients—the brokers themselves—tried the software and saw it indeed worked and realized they could take their clients' up-to-date data home with them every night, the decision was an instantaneous "yes." Could the broker pay for it? Of course, immediately, by personal check. In practice, payment was in 30 days, and Alpaca had no problems with cash flow. It did have to issue new stock, though, because as it was addressing the real need of the worthiest clients, its revenue growth approached 100 percent a year, and it needed money to finance it.

Now, why did I say that Alpaca's clients were the worthiest imaginable? Because they combined all the qualities you would look for when you sleuth. They had high personal income, nearly all of it was tied to their job performance, which the product was directly affecting, the payoff was to them personally, they had the power to make a decision, and they had the money to pay for it.

It was at this stage that I went to meet management once again and found them paragons of hard work and honesty. I also scouted the nearby food emporia to see where corporate personnel are likely to come to unwind. They rarely did—they worked nearly nonstop—but the coffee shop across the road was one where some could often be found. I chatted with a few, made a few discreet inquiries about background of employees, and of the financiers behind Alpaca, and eventually bought its stock—quite a bit of it—and put it into clients' accounts.

Then, to my surprise, came the company's second growth stage. Once brokers in a brokerage firm's branch bought Alpaca's software, the poor upper manager *had* to buy the controlling piece of software that would sit on the brokerage firm's own servers and view the data on the individual brokers' PCs, or the brokers could leave with the firm's assets on a disk. As a result, Alpaca's growth *accelerated*.

ALEXANDRINE STRATEGY

By that time, my firm's clients and I had about a fourfold gain in the stock, so I was keeping tabs on the company via its customers (the brokers) nearly every week, to make sure I did not miss the time to sell. However, the fundamentals only kept getting better and better. It was also at this stage that Alpaca executed one of the most brilliant corporate strategies possible—one invented by Alexander the Great and named after him: In essence, a *direct frontal attack* on the opponent's *strongest* point. (Please note that this is also what you'd be doing when you get between a company and its clients, to force management to pay attention to you.) Alexander used to attack at the enemy's strongest point because that was often the least defended, and once you managed to breach it, the enemy often crumbled.

Alpaca made a beeline to confront CRM's biggest player—Laird—taking aim at Laird's best and most prestigious clients: Wall Street super-brokers, such as Morgan Stanley, Goldman Sachs, Merrill Lynch, and others. Alpaca's management knew, of course, that it would be hard to gain a toehold there. But it also knew that if it managed to draw these top-notch customers away, Laird would have to acquire Alpaca at a high price—just to get their customers back.

It was a daring strategy, as is the sleuthing strategy of getting close to a company's main clients, but it was also a logical one because Laird, whose software was (in my view) inferior, was serving mostly Wall Street whip-masters rather than the brokers. The inevitable result was that Laird began to hemorrhage Wall Street top broker-clients to Alpaca. Its stock momentum began to falter and Alpaca's stock rise accelerated further.

All this I learned by calling brokers and brokerage offices' back-office administrators. At that point I, too, had an Alpaca CRM module myself, to keep track of my informers and others I sleuthed, their photos, topics we had talked of before, and their connections to other informants. It was during one of these chats with brokers that I learned that Alpaca was offering to install CRM in the Midwestern regional office of a national firm as proof the software could be installed in the firm's other offices later on. This was momentous—and I would never have heard about it had I not kept in touch with Alpaca's broker-customers on a regular basis.

What I found out was that the software was installed against significant opposition by Laird's headquarters, but supported by a progressive whip-master at the local brokerage office—perhaps helped by pressure from some rebellious brokers. At any rate, once Alpaca's software was installed, the brokers-users' response was most enthusiastic. (I talked to three, and after that, others began to call me.) However, facing the risk of losing the entire national firm's software account, Laird allegedly panicked. The apocryphal story (which came to me thirdhand) was that a top executive at Laird called the brokerage firm's top New York honchos and said, in effect, "You aren't going to hand over the personal details of all of your clients to a bunch of Socialist Canadians who speak French and ride dog-sleds." The next day, a directive came from the national brokerage's headquarters in New York to its Midwestern office instructing them to dig out the Alpaca system and switch back over to Laird. There was an alleged rebellion in the ranks (which I heard about secondhand from a back-office lady with whom I had become friendly some months before). One story (again, unconfirmed) was that some high-level brokers threatened to leave if Alpaca's system was not kept.

VICTORY FOR THE DESERVING

That very night there was jubilation in the coffee shop across the road from Alpaca's head office in Toronto, where I sat for my weekly coffee. One did not have to hear the salespeople's words (I didn't) to realize from their jubilant tone there was a chance the contract would be retained. And indeed, calls to the Midwestern brokerage branch the next day indicated that Laird was caving. Later, when all was over, I learned that two days after the branch threw out the Laird system in favor of Alpaca's under pressure by the brokers, Laird executives flew to Toronto and within a few weeks made a takeover offer for all of Alpaca's stock, at a valuation of close to $1.5 billion for revenues of a mere $75 million. It represented about 20 times our original cost. Of course, we didn't get the full profit by then because we had been selling stock all through its rise, out of prudence. As a final note, Laird allegedly closed down Alpaca within a year and moved the brokers-clients back to its own system.

From my point of view, Alpaca was as near perfect an investment as possible. What can you learn from it, and how can you duplicate such a success story? Here are the obvious main lessons:

- When analyzing a company whose stock you find cheap, don't start with the company or its financials, its product, or its market. Start with the clients and ask yourself, "Are they worth serving?" This is a typical sleuth question—customers first, everything else later.

- Look for companies who sell directly to triple-decision makers. The closer the customer's decision makers are to the ideal profile, the more money you can make by investing in the company that serves them.

- The faster the decision-making cycle, the better.

- Never forget that some customers are worth serving, and some aren't. So just by nixing investments in stocks of companies who sell to committees of clerks, you will increase the productivity of your sleuthing manyfold—and raise your chances of getting rich.

WHEN YOU GET RICH

And now allow me to execute a little detour, because when you get rich, the above categories of check senders can be extremely useful to you. Let me provide some examples to show you how you can handle your own wealth like a corporation handles its cash.

Since check-sending is such a crucial corporate activity, any smart corporation divides it into three parts, as you have seen. However, these three categories of corporate check senders—*ownership, control,* and *benefit*—conform very closely to the three money management functions you yourself must separate when you start managing your own accumulating pile of wealth.

When you are poor, or at least not wealthy, you automatically mix these three functions together and perform them all under your own name. You own the cash in your bank or brokerage account under your own name, you control it by signing your own name on checks, and you benefit directly from the cash by buying a car or a home, which you own under your name or your spouse's. There is a convenience in this merging of functions, but there are also risks and costs. In fact, truly rich people always separate these three money functions, so as to minimize taxes, immunize themselves against lawsuits, divorce claims, estate taxes, and others perils of wealth. They also gain other benefits, such as flexibility, anonymity, and security. And as you grow richer, as you likely will, once you invest like a sleuth, you too will gain such benefits.

How exactly is it done? It is done by separating wealth ownership from its control and its benefits.

The cash, or stocks, or property, you accumulate can be *owned* by a holding company or a trust, where *control* of the money can be held formally by a lawyer (whom you kindly advise and pay), or by trustees (one of whom is you), while the *beneficiaries* can be yourself, your spouse, children, or anyone else you or your trustees designate—your alma mater, or the local orphanage. Indeed, rich people have been known to start trusts just as poorer people open bank accounts.

Now, it is not my intention to provide here a personal financial planning manual. However, I do feel a sense of obligation to mention this, because once you start investing according to the methods in this book, you are likely to start accumulating large sums of capital at a rapid clip. And if you have never handled large amounts of money before, this can be a shock (I have seen it happen), both because of the sudden lavish possibilities and because of the sudden claims that others can and will make upon your new wealth, if you own it and control it outright and personally. So if I teach you how to make large amounts of money, without at least mentioning the basics of handling it, I might be causing you inadvertent grief, just as if I had handed to you a Ferrari Dino 250 or a Lamborghini Bora (both of which you may soon be able to afford), without teaching you first how to drive such a high-powered beast.

Any good commercial lawyer would be happy to sell you an hour or two of his or her time to elaborate on the subject. But back to the topic of stock-sleuthing ...

As a wealthy individual, or family, you'd like to separate these three money functions as much as possible, as well as distance them from yourself. However, the ideal *business*, from your perpective as a stock investor, is one whose *customers* do *not* separate these three functions, so that the company has direct contact and access to their single-function check sender. This way *the vendor—the company in whose stock you invest*—will have more control over its customers' cash (via the check senders) than the check sender's bosses.

In the case of Alpaca, you saw how the above principle translated to one of the most perfect stock investments ever. It can do the same for you once you apply it in your own sleuthing.

CHAPTER

THE COMPANY'S SUPPLIERS

U
ntil now we've concentrated on two types of people: those who work for the company, and the customers or check senders. We've endeavored to learn who they are, why they do what they do, and how they do it—both individually and together. The objective in both these types of sleuthing is to understand the *routine* business of the company, whether it concerns the internal operations or the external flow of checks. Both of these are critical for long-term investors.

However, when you sleuth the third category of people—those who work for the company's suppliers—your focus will be on *disruptions* of routine activities. This is where you try to discover *changes in the ordinary business flow*, positive or negative. With this information you can either identify budding turnarounds for investment or coming disasters that can be shorted profitably.

As you've probably concluded, if sleuthing to understand a business's routine is more useful for long-term investors, the search for clues to sudden changes (such as a gain or loss of big contracts, coming mass resignations of key people, or a coming takeover) is usually performed by traders for a one-time gain. Such sleuths are often romantic souls enamored of action, willing to work more and pay higher taxes (since short-duration ownerships and short sales may not qualify for capital gains), for the sheer fun of it. Yet even long-term investors should be acquainted with this branch of sleuthing, because even the best long-term investment can occasionally suffer massive short-term disruptions, and these can often be foreseen via the suppliers' employees. Conversely, this kind of sleuthing can also uncover some good companies that suffered temporary setbacks, and whose cheap stocks may be on the verge of mending. So let's dig deeper into this type of sleuthing.

PRODUCT SUPPLIERS

In any business, there are two kinds of suppliers: those that supply products and those that provide services. We discuss product suppliers first and service suppliers later in the chapter. For example, if XYZ makes microchips, it would buy machinery to melt the silicon (or buy silicon slabs ready made), special saws to cut the slabs, chemicals to polish them, ion implanters to stick impurities into the surface, photo-masks to draw the circuit upon the impregnated surface, and so on. Each component is an ingredient in the final product.

The key difference between most investors and sleuths is that most investors, including those who run mutual funds, even hedge funds, view themselves as stock *scientists*. Stock sleuths, on the other hand, see themselves as *field operatives*. What rarely occurs to stock scientists is that you can track product components *physically*—where they are made, when they are shipped, and how many are shipped. Then, if you know the price, which you can get by calling the company's salespeople and asking for a quote, you can compute the sales revenues such volume is expected to deliver. And if you know these facts—which admittedly can be tedious and lengthy to obtain—you can get a somewhat precise estimate of XYZ's business volume. This is not an activity to be engaged in lightly, but at critical junctures, it can give you a great edge over the stock scientists.

You can also obtain similar estimates for XYZ plant expansions, since such plans often require municipal licenses for discharging efflu-ents and investment by local government in additional infrastructure. Checking with the local municipality may yield little or no informa-tion, or, as happened to me more than once, you can find a detailed forecast by the company of its future needs, including five years of pro-jections, by quarter.

The above example assumes XYZ produces physical products such as microchips. But what if you are looking at an entire industry? This is far trickier, because it can lead you into the dangerous world of theory and interpretation of public data from the comfort of your home or office, where stock scientists dwell. But if you keep your feet firmly planted on the physical ground, there are quite a number of techniques you can use to get the information you need. The first and simplest is that of *physical counting*. Before I provide you with an actual example, please take note that none other than the Russian novelist Leo Tolstoy mentions it in his great novel *Anna Karenina*.

In that book (Part 2, chapter 17), the dissolute Prince Oblonksy sells his forest to a wood merchant, Ryabinin, for a third of its real value because Oblonsky is a lazy aristocrat who never bothered to learn the for-est's true value *by counting the trees*. When a friend—the virtuous hero Lyovin—asks him why he didn't bother to determine how many trees are in the forest, Oblonsky says disdainfully that noblemen don't count trees. So Lyovin notes sarcastically that because Oblonsky didn't count his trees and the merchant did, the latter's children would go to good schools, while those of Oblonsky would not.

What Tolstoy implies is that neglecting to learn what one's property is really worth and selling it too cheaply is truly a sin against one's family. The same point can be made about many office-bound investors who do not *physically* examine what they invest in, preferring to play with math-ematical formulas and logic instead. This allows others to make the profit, which of course can include you. And now for an actual case of counting supplies ...

COUNT PHYSICAL UNITS ON A LARGE
SCALE BY TRACKING THE SUPPLIERS

A good friend of mine, whom I'll call Paul, runs one of the most successful funds in the world, and he has become very interested in uranium. His assistant, who is of Russian descent, read a note in some regional Russian newspapers that the Russian government was exploring for uranium to use in their nuclear reactors. Paul knew that the Russians had been dismantling atom bombs to extract the cores for their nuclear reactors, and because the Russians were supposed to have many such bombs, this had suggested that they had a plentiful supply. However, that they were continuing exploration for uranium suggested that it was actually in scarce supply. Since identifying a true imbalance between supply and demand is often the surest way to make a fortune, Paul decided to check this out—physically. But how?

Paul immersed himself in the economics of uranium. He and his assistant prepared a list of *nearly every nuclear plant in the world*, including each one's source of supply, the electrical output and the metal input, the cost of uranium as a percentage of the plants' operating costs, and the names of the top management and personnel at each plant. Then he did the same for uranium mines and so on down the pipeline.

Paul visited several plants around the world. He talked to midlevel employees and established warm personal relations with several. His assistant established connections with a few more. Paul then met with government regulatory agencies, with uranium processors, and with analysts. The latter had very little to add to the physical data, but they knew names of uranium producers and had information about their expansion plans.

For obvious reasons, Paul kept his data under lock and key. After a few good months of sleuthing, he and his assistant began the physical inventory of uranium: how much was being produced and where, how much was being consumed and by whom, how much was planned to be produced in the future, where and for whom. They prepared a huge table with all the data, then Paul and his assistant took a random sample of points from the table and traveled to check the accuracy by physically counting tonnage at mines or supplies at reactors. The latter was tricky, but by that time management at the nuclear reactors knew Paul was reliable. Moreover, by now he was in a position to give them information they did not have (just as I did with the management of Smalltech; see Chapter 2).

Paul also tracked contracts for physical supplies of other materials and services to reactors—especially those whose volumes were proportional to the consumption of uranium. Whereas reactor personnel are often twitchy about uranium supply data, physical data about ancillary products and services are often more easily available. Suffice it to say that, as a result, he could produce very reliable data about the physical demand for uranium in the civilian market.

Once this process was over, Paul and his assistant finalized their tables. These were meticulous, detailed, and large. Each item was cross-correlated and the source of information noted. At that point, the table was shown to a few government experts who were asked to comment on their accuracy. Most were astonished. No one had done such work before. The supply and demand relationship was clear and pointed in one direction— a supply shortage.

Furthermore, if military demand for uranium for new nuclear weapons was to be added to civilian demand, the shortage would be even steeper. And because oil was also in short supply and little new oil was being found, the only reasonably priced alternative was nuclear power. The uranium shortage, in other words, would only increase.

Contrary to the approach of most sleuths, who target individual companies (which is what I strongly recommend), the results of Paul's sleuthing did not pertain to a specific company, but rather to the detailed, *physical* supply situation of uranium worldwide. He looked at it mine by mine, country by country, reactor by reactor, proven and probable reserves, producers, political situation in every producing country, and where mines were about to go into production.

It took seven months to compile these details; however, once assembled, the information convinced Paul that the uranium supply and demand situation was so out of balance that prices were likely to rise steeply, especially since more reactors were being built (he had filing cabinets with detailed lists of these, including who would build them). And inasmuch as uranium costs were 8 to 10 percent of reactor operating costs, whereas shutting down a reactor would cost billions, even if uranium prices doubled or tripled electricity prices would not be unduly increased and, therefore, not crimp demand.

Paul loaded up on uranium stocks and kept loading even as the price rose. So far, he has been correct.

When will he sell, you ask? His physical tracking will tell him. Or, as he jokingly says, he would likely start selling when either a popular business or investment magazine did a cover story on uranium, because that's when the stock scientists, who operate on screen data and print information, would come onboard.

How can *you* use physical sleuthing? What if you are interested in a mundane company or a mundane product? You should be happy to hear that such companies often provide the most fertile ground for physical sleuthing through their suppliers—and the more mundane the better.

MUNDANE PRODUCTS OFTEN
ARE THE EASIEST TO TRACK

For example, say that XYZ is a producer of frozen pizza that is packaged in large cardboard boxes printed with pictures of smiling jolly chefs and sold in supermarkets. The company is publicly traded, but the stock has been a ho-hum investment for years—no new products, very high costs (due to an abundance of nonproductive family members onboard), high employee turnover, and perhaps a scandal or two. You found the stock very cheap, but always gave it a pass because of the entrenched bad management. However, let's say you have just heard that enterprising new managers bought the old family out, came in, and are cutting costs. They are also letting the idle old guard go, spending on new products (microwavable pizza), and steadily buying stock in the market.

As a sidebar, note that one of the most fertile grounds for sleuths is a list of cheap stocks where control changed hands or new management has arrived and is shaking things up. You can have a friendly broker do a text search for you via the Bloomberg service looking for new CEOs, then check for cheapness. Or you can scan the 13D filings in *Barron's* or on the SEC's Edgar site for creeping change of control or activist investors (see Chapter 8).

But back to the sleuthing part. How can you find out XYZ's own internal estimate or forecast for the future? This sort of data is what a money manager would kill for, and the type that, if secretly shared by an executive with an investor, would constitute insider information for which both could go to jail. Yet there are ways to find such forecasts safely, surely, and legally. How?

PHYSICAL CLUES ARE KEY TO FORECASTING

A sleuth would first learn the product's *physical ingredients*. Say you check with the pizza chef at the corner pizza store and learn that the ingredients are cheese, flour, yeast, dried vegetables, oil, and cardboard boxes. You check further and identify who the main suppliers are of each of these items. Since flour, yeast, and oil are all sold in bulk and stored inside the company, they cannot provide you much visual information. However, the cardboard boxes are another matter—like most items produced by smaller suppliers, they have a one-to-one relationship to product volume. That is, one product sold equals one supply item used.

This is why a sleuth would immediately zero in on the cardboard boxes as potentially the best bet for outside information. And, as you'll discover once you start doing it, much of product packaging made for a company by outside suppliers can occasionally be observed and counted away from the company's premises.

So assume you found out where the company buys its cardboard boxes. If it's a small manufacturer, you can check to see where the boxes are stored, and whether you can see them from across the street. Better still, you may be able to count them. Or, if you can't, is it possible to chat with some employees at the box manufacturer? If the box manufacturer is not publicly traded, you have more leeway for gathering information. Or, how about the printer that stamps the boxes with the image of the jolly chef? Perhaps you can get some physical indication there about the volume they deliver? Ingenuity, similar to that displayed by the sleuth's secretary who found the caterer in the LBO example (see Chapter 1), can help you determine the volume that the printer or the box maker can deliver by asking about their other customers.

In all this, check with your lawyer about what you can and cannot ask. But you'll find that you can do much more than you might initially imagine, especially when you keep firmly in mind that you are looking for primary *physical* information, not secondhand data.

In my experience, packaging can often provide the best indication of volume. That, and finding out the precise manufacturing process. If you know the latter and can find out what the volume bottlenecks are, you can often track when these are reached by knowing which employees are required at each stage of the process.

Once again, one of the common threads running through this book is the advice to think in concrete, physical terms. Unlike financial analysts who are taught to think about symbols and relationships among symbols (the financial statements), and unlike technical analysts who are taught to think in terms of price squiggles and their derivatives (such as moving averages), I advise you to go to the physical reality behind all of these representations. Go physical, *always*. Once you start, you'll realize that very few investors see investments in physical terms, so your competition for such information will be slim, and your chance for exclusivity very high.

One note about the process: In Chapter 4 we'll see how tracking the product's physical supplies can often forecast sudden changes in volume quite accurately. But since, in most cases, people who work for the physical suppliers are several steps removed from the customer, it's not necessary to pay as much attention to them as to those who provide intangible supplies or services.

To show this in a specific example, remember the stock sleuth who learned that an LBO company used a French restaurant to cater a dinner before every important deal? To find out when such deals took place, he had his secretary sit in front of the LBO company's office waiting for the chef to arrive. She could also have tailed the chef until he finally had a delivery to make at the LBO's office, but it was far more economical for her to sit in front of the premises and wait for the caterer's truck to arrive than to follow him around town. This, in fact, is an old principle in intelligence work. Don't tail the opponent all over town unless you think he's going to meet other people of interest. It is much better to stay near his destination, if you know it, and wait for him to come to you.

There are times, however, when it is better to watch the supplies rather than the supplier. It is rumored that Israeli intelligence used to periodically survey the warehouse of a towel factory in an Arab capital that supplied antiseptic towels to army hospitals. If any large hostilities were being planned, Army field hospitals would put in a large store of towels, and the factory would fill up with boxes and packages. Of course, such an event would rarely occur, but when it did, it was crucial to learn of it, as it could trigger orders. And informants could cross-check for other extra supplies being stored. How to find out about the towels? Well, the factory warehouse's broken windows afforded an excellent view of the shelves inside. A common laborer passing by and looking idly in, once a day, could glimpse this key data without attracting attention. Physical surveillance, as we noted before, is often simpler than one thinks.

Similarly, if you find out where a supplier stores its items before it ships them to XYZ, and if its warehouse is visible from the road outside, you can either pass by there yourself periodically—or pay a local to watch it for you and tell you when supplies pile up. Likewise, you should try to find out if supplies are being unloaded on a shipping dock where they can be visually counted, either by you or by someone else assisting you.

SERVICE SUPPLIERS

But aside from cases such as the above, where physical supplies tied to production are easily tracked from outside the company, the stock sleuth is best advised to track the *people* who provide *services* to XYZ. And the best of those are often the professionals—accountants, lawyers, or bankers. Especially the kind of bankers who provide what can be termed "services of sudden change"—takeover planning, mergers and acquisitions, or loan restructuring.

RECOGNIZING SUPPLIERS' KEY PERSONNEL

Here is the sort of advice you have probably not seen elsewhere or ever heard about in business school. When we advise you to track things physically, we also mean to track people. Know who the important ones are and, at the important junctions, track them. This advice I provide with great trepidation, because it is not my intention to have you stalk corporate or banking executives all over town around the clock. Furthermore, regular tailing of such personnel would yield you very little—most have routines that do not vary much. However, the clients they meet are often worth your attention, because they are executives whose companies either need emergency financing or are planning to merge with another company, sell their own company, or buy another.

This is why, if you want to make money by anticipating takeovers, mergers, or corporate restructuring, you must get to know the faces of the main advisors for such activities in your locale. And by "get to know," I mean to be able to recognize them, as well as know where they live, where they work, what their clubs are, their social, educational, and work background, and all other details you would collect about executives of companies in whose stock you are interested.

Why do you need all that info about the financial service providers? For the simple reason that you want to be able to recognize them when they pass you in the street, anytime, anywhere. They may be walking along with one or two other people in business suits, and at such a time you want to be able to whip out your camera cell phone and snap quick two or three pictures and e-mail these to your office, to be perused later. Even if in only one case out of five, the gunslinger's companions are chatting about a live takeover or a merger, this one occasional photograph can be worth quite a bit of money for you. (And yes, keep the photo on file and drop yourself a quick memo to file about how and when you took it, with a copy to your lawyer.)

Or, say you happen to see the premier takeover merchant banker in town breaking bread with the premier takeover lawyer in town, alongside three anonymous executives whom you do not recognize. What then? Yes, out comes your camera cell phone, and you snap a picture of the group. Ditto if you see the VP of corporate development (which is another name for acquisitions) for XYZ chatting quietly in an airport bar with suited professionals.

As a side note, tracking "persons of interest" is what most intelligence services do, to gather clues about these persons' intentions and plans. If a known terrorist has met an unknown man in Jakarta, that unknown man gets photographed immediately and his photo circulated to try to identify him. If he's identified as a radical student of country Y, that country's security service is promptly notified of a potential impending event. People's associations and those they meet can provide plenty of information—both in the field of intelligence and in the field of finance.

Now, since your resources are far more modest than those of an intelligence service, and you aren't qualified to follow people and track their movements, this is not something I recommend that you do. However, you should be able to identify the main mergers and acquisitions (M&A) players in your town, both inside companies you have an interest in and outside them.

Knowing who these players are is easier than you think. Even if you live in a smaller town, there always are the select few professionals—whether they work for the local bank, brokerage firm, or accounting firm—who are the most active in buying and selling businesses. In fact, one of the most useful data items a sleuth can have is a collection of photographs of local investment bankers and lawyers and accountants who are involved in most mergers, acquisitions, and takeovers in town. If you say that this is impractical, and that you could not possibly be expected to remember faces of strangers, think again. First, you don't have to follow all companies and all stocks. If you follow technology stocks exclusively, there are only half a dozen firms behind the majority of the large deals. If you concentrate on forestry companies or small banks, there are specialists who handle them too. Once you start reading the professional publications of that industry, you can zero in on the mergers, both the large and the small, and track down which law firms, accounting firms, or brokerage firms helped in the transactions. To then get the names of those who participated, you only have to show some initiative. But then what?

GET PHOTOGRAPHS OF THE
SERVICE SUPPLIERS' PEOPLE

Get as many photographs as you can of the important service suppliers and learn to identify them. Surely you can identify at least 20 movie stars, and perhaps at least as many TV personalities, and half a dozen golf pros, just as your children can recognize dozens of the latest teen-movie idols and sports superstars. In fact, most people can probably recognize several dozen faces of people with whom they have no social contact and who provide them no income. If you can recognize strangers' faces that do not make you or your kin any money, why couldn't you take the trouble to memorize faces of the active finance stars in your town or in the area of the stock market where you have an interest? Similarly, it would pay you to memorize the faces of the main executives of companies headquartered in your town and the faces of their directors, most of which you can get from annual reports or by snapping pictures of them at the annual meeting.

SEE YOURSELF AS A BUSINESS FAN

Getting to know the movers and shakers of the industry by sight is the first step to knowing who is doing what to whom. Getting to know their background will also give you a glimpse into the "why." This, too, is something that all intelligence services and agents do as a matter of course. They snap pictures of members of the opposition, whom they either follow or happen to see, as well as those with whom these opposing members meet. Intelligence services capture all this data in huge databases, similar to that of fictitious Alpaca we investigated in Chapter 2, only on a much larger and much more elaborate scale. Unless you have something similar, you'll probably have to rely on your memory or that of your family members and friends or members of your investment club whom you co-opted.

And here is advice that may sound esoteric, but is actually quite practical. There are some rare people who have a photographic memory. They can remember faces and names and many other details nearly forever, after seeing them only once. In the days before computers came into being, the Russian, the Israeli, and the British secret services were rumored to employ such people, not always in an organized manner, but on an ad hoc basis. Today most of data tracking is, of course, automated. But if you are in the money management business or are a member of an investment club and you happen to find a person with a photographic memory, no matter what age or other ability, hire or recruit him or her. Or, get people in your investment club to help. If they can identify even one executive who dined with the anti-takeover lawyer, it would be well worth the effort. Some other business stars, such as special accountants and special PR people, often appear when a company is about to be taken over. If you manage to find out who these business stars are, you could be on your way to discovering the next takeover target. The same advice applies to lawyers who specialize in corporate bankruptcies if you prefer shorting pending disasters.

GETTING PICTURES

In the past it was harder to obtain photographs of the deal makers in your town, since they weren't generally featured in corporate documents. You had to track down graduation photos whose youthful faces might not be a good current representation, or you could engage in surreptitious photography in such locales as restaurants or annual meetings. Both activities are perfectly legal, but because of the old bulky equipment, they might have made you seem conspicuous.

With the advent of the Internet, it is far easier to find photos of M&A stars. Law firms often put pictures of their key players on their website, and brokerage firms occasionally do the same. Another rich source of photographs is the society pages, which feature glossy photos of galas where the cream of the local commercial crop have danced the night away to support this or that medical or social cause. Clipping such pictures should be a habit for any sleuth.

As for which law or banking firms do what, and which business stars deserve to have their photos in your file cabinet, professional lawyers' magazines occasionally announce which law firm was involved in what deal and financial newspapers occasionally feature pieces about lawyers or brokers whose prowess in deal-making merit recognition, or showcase famous forensic accountants whose mere presence in a corporation indicates the possibility that some fraud was discovered.

ANNUAL RANKINGS OFTEN REVEAL THE STARS

Every year, ranked lists of various brokerage firms' involvement in takeovers, mergers, and acquisitions are published. If you are interested in this sort of deal-making as a way of anticipating price movements, you should build a database tracking lawyers and investment bankers who are involved in such activities. Over time, you'll begin to discern which law and brokerage firms get involved in which kind of deals. For example, Allen and Company in New York City has often been involved in media companies' mergers. Broadview Associates (today Jeffries-Broadview) is most often the lead investment banker in software acquisitions. Some firms specialize in regional bank mergers, of which there are often quite a few small deals a year, while others are specialists that make their living advising other industries' mergers. If you find out who they are and learn to recognize them, all you need is one or two *physical* indications of a coming deal to make a profit. The questions you should ask are the following:

- Who are the top advisors who do the deals in the area of your interest?

- What do they look like? Where do they live? What cars do they drive?

- Who are their senior associates? Their assistants? Secretaries?

- Where do they work? Which other professionals do they often work with?

Learn who all of these people are; get to know their faces, their backgrounds, their hobbies, their office locations, as if you are a VP of sales and these are potential clients. Admittedly, this sort of data is easier to gather and track if you are a money manager or a professional investor with some office help. But even if you are an amateur, or a member of an investment club, you can perform some of it. You'll certainly be doing what few other investors do.

RISKS

Now what can you do with this kind of photographic and personal information? Here is where you can tread on tricky ground, because this sort of tracking requires some expertise, and if you want to sleuth legal personnel engaged in M&A, you can easily become a target if you do anything that can be deemed as stalking or harassment. Finally, you can end up wasting your time, without getting any useful leads.

For example, if you know the locations of your town's high-profile M&A lawyers or merchant bankers, it is not difficult to station yourself in front of the office building to see who they lunch with or return to their office with. Or, especially at the close of the business day, what people they leave the building with, engaged in the tail end of apparent business discussions.

Such close tracking is not—repeat, *not*—recommended as routine activity. It can be profitable only when you have in mind a specific event you are trying to forecast, *and* if you have someone on your team both experienced in such activities and with ongoing access to legal advice. As in all sleuthing activities, always keep in your mind the potential benefit against the potential cost, both in time and in aggravation.

To put this all into perspective, and to highlight the fact that sleuthing a location is better than skulking after people, here is an example where such physical tracking produced a profit. It should give you an idea about what you, too, can do.

SLEUTHING FINANCIAL-SERVICE SUPPLIERS FROM AN OBSERVATION POST

I met "Michelle" when we were both MBA students. She was Canadian too and, as a math graduate, was convinced that stocks moved according to a scientific formula that one could discover by research. So, of course, she lost money in fistfuls in her forays into the market. This, in fact, as she told me, was why she came to business school—to learn how to invest profitably. Unfortunately, her studies, which centered on mathematical finance, taught her that you can't make more money than others in stocks without taking on more risk, and so only ensured she'd lose more. I still remember the famous business school joke: Professor Bill Sharpe is walking down Wall Street with Warren Buffett, when suddenly both see a dollar bill lying on the ground. When Buffett bends to pick it up, Professor Sharpe tells him not to bother, because surely the dollar isn't there, or someone would have picked it up before.

This about sums up efficient market theory—only it's expressed in math, where risk is not equated with ignorance but, strangely, with the squiggliness of the price line (called "volatility"). Despite this silly notion of risk, half the MBA class who took mathematical finance courses believed in EMT in its various forms, strong and weak, especially the engineers and math graduates. At any rate, when the two years of MBA coursework were finished, I returned to Toronto to work as a stock analyst, while Michelle stayed behind at Stanford to earn a PhD in mathematical finance. When she received her doctorate two years later, she went to Toronto, where, because of her degree and pedigree, she was grabbed immediately by the Canadian subsidiary of a U.S. bank that started an index fund and put Michelle's PhD to work.

MARKET INDEX—A MEASUREMENT
OF MEDIOCRITY

A market index is a collection of stocks that have become famous and high-priced enough to be included in an official stock list that major institutions that run billions can buy, like the 30 Dow Jones Industrials, or the S&P 500, or the NASDAQ 100. The hidden shame of most big money managers is that a majority of them do worse than such passive indices. Why? My belief is that it's because they buy only famous and expensive stocks that analysts talk up in order to help the company sell new stock. Then the same big money managers sell the same erstwhile-famous stocks on the downswing when they become disgraced and cheap. This is what happened in the tech bubble and still takes place today.

However, this is only my view. Index-fund devotees, on the other hand, say that the majority of money managers do worse than the market averages because they *can't* do better without "inside information"—as proven by EMT. (Like Warren's Buffett's found-dollar which "can't" be there.) So don't even try to pick stocks, the indexers say. Just put your retirement savings into a collection of the most famous stocks, and you'll beat four out of five active managers. To me, this is like financial communism: don't compete because it doesn't pay. So just join the herd and be average.

COMMUNISM OF THE STOCK MARKET

Just as Communism appeals to the naïve and idealistic, so do index funds appeal to the same type of persons in the market, of which there are many. So the market index fund Michelle worked for grew. Her work involved smoothing out trading fluctuations, minimizing trading commissions, and assuring those who bought the index fund that it would mimic the market index's rise and fall closely. For Michelle, who was a kind and liberal soul, there was also a feeling of a mission of helping the masses invest their hard-earned savings, safe from promotional brokers' analysts and incompetent money managers who suckered investors with the false promise of doing better than the market.

Michelle's office was a few floors below the rooftop gym to which I belonged, and so I saw her occasionally in the elevator. We had lunch once or twice, reminisced about Stanford, and argued about the stock market. She said that trying to find cheap stocks was deluded, because all information was in the price already, as proven by science. I said to her that her "science" was not only wrong, but it was also silly. Are stock investments, I asked, the only commercial occupation known to humankind where brains and hard work were not enough to earn more than others without taking on needless risk? In short, we agreed to disagree.

About a year later, after I had already been money sleuthing for six months, I saw Michelle sitting on one of the benches in front of the Toronto Dominion Bank tower, staring straight ahead, apparently distraught. I stopped and asked her what was wrong

She replied that she had just made $90,000 in the market.

I am afraid I laughed out loud and said that it must have been random. But the look she gave me was pained. "No!" she said. "It wasn't random, and now I feel stupid. Because if I could make money like this, what's my PhD worth?" I told her I would buy her coffee if she would tell me what she had done. She agreed, and we descended to the underground food court, and there, over a double latte, she told me how she had made $90,000 in the market in a week. How did she do it? She sleuthed, of course.

BUSINESS AS A DAILY SOAP OPERA

Across the hall from Michelle's office was a department of one of Canada's major banks, which I shall call here the Bank of Industry (B of I). Michelle got to know a few of their people, and she eventually learned that this particular department was in charge of loan workouts.

Essentially, if a company to whom the B of I had loaned money could not pay it back, the bank either forced the borrower to cut costs so that the loan could be repaid, or if this were not enough, the bank sometimes sold the company for whatever it could bring and got as much of its loan back as it could, even if the owners were left with nothing. Just like your bank selling your house if you can't meet the mortgage payments. In rare cases, however, the bank reduced the amount it was owed—this was called a loan "haircut"—which also reduced the interest payments and gave the borrower some breathing room. A haircut usually helped a borrower regain its health and even prosper—in which case the bank often participated though warrants to buy stock.

The impact of a workout on an indebted company's share price, if the company was public, was immediate: its shares usually soared. (If the bank holding your mortgage agreed to cut the amount you owe it, your net worth would jump too.) If, on the other hand, the bank forced the company to pay, in the same way a bank foreclosed on your home, the price of the debtor's shares, equivalent to your net worth, declined also. When Michelle learned what that B of I's department across the hall did, she began to follow its people's comings and goings with sharp interest, because, let's face it, her own work was not the most exciting. Thus, she often saw despondent executives come in, shoulders bowed, while the bank's financial Rambos herded the newcomers through the door, winking at each other while maintaining grave faces. The bank's negotiators were all seasoned pros, and the chance of them taking a haircut on behalf of the bank was low. But occasionally it happened.

The year Michelle started her job, a publicly traded advertising agency had borrowed $10,000,000 from the B of I, only to see their largest clients drop them and render them unable to pay back the loan. When the bank asked the agency's CFO to cut costs, the ad executives threatened to take the company into bankruptcy and then all resign en masse together with the copywriters, unless the bank relented.

An ad agency without its execs and creative personnel is next to worthless, so the bank's negotiating leverage was nil. Its only option was to take a haircut on its loan and help the agency get back on its feet. The question was only how much of a haircut. The negotiations lasted a week, and finally the bank relented. The day the news of the loan "restructuring" hit the Bloomberg news, the ad company's depressed shares jumped 50 percent. Michelle always remembered this as she watched the daily parade of despondent borrowers being greeted at the elevator by the B of I's loan officers, whose job it was to either lower the boom or, reluctantly and rarely, forgive a portion of their loans.

LUCKY FLY ON THE CEILING

Michelle told me that more than once she had daydreamed of being a fly on the wall of the meeting room where the workout decisions were made. Because if it was a public company whose loan was being renegotiated, the decision could mean that the next day the stock would move either down or up depending on the bank's decision to squeeze or relent. Of course, there was no way of learning this in advance—unless one was a bank insider or an insider of the borrower. And if one was either, one could not buy or sell stock on the information without risk of prosecution. On this, Michelle was clear. Yet she dreamed about it, maybe because her training was based on the "scientific proof" that you can't beat the market. So she kept watching the soap opera across the hall, even as she worked at creating perfectly average investments.

Then one morning she noted that the coterie of executives emerging out of the elevator were uncommonly self-confident, while the nervous ones this time were the bank officers who greeted them at the elevator. Michelle could see them all through the glass partition of her office, which overlooked her company's reception with its glass front doors. She had looked through these double glass partitions many times before, and was used to seeing nervous newcomers and confident bankers. Only this time the roles seemed reversed.

Because this was unusual behavior, she was intrigued, and, acting on instinct, she left her office and went, ostensibly, to the washroom, but really to observe what was going on from up close. A little crowd was jostling each other through the bank department's front door, clutching briefcases and newspapers. Michelle sauntered by and glanced at the briefcases to see if any had a business card in an airline tag attached—but there was nothing. The newspapers might have had the name of the subscriber and his company printed on the corner—but there was nothing either. Then the little crowd went inside the bank entrance and disappeared.

CARPE DIEM

Michelle lingered a minute, then returned to her office, where she pretended to work, but really stared through the glass partitions waiting for the meeting at the B of I to end. A little before noon, the visiting executives strode out, with the bank's executives slouching dejectedly behind them. One did not have to be a master sleuth to recognize what had just taken place. Michelle was out of her chair in a flash; she waited for the crowd at the elevator's door, and joined them on their way down. They seemed to bubble with suppressed excitement. Michelle scrutinized them surreptitiously, desperately trying to see any identifying sign of the company they worked for—and then she saw it. A red-and-white logo on the shirt-protector of one of the engineers—the well-known emblem of a commercial animation company, let's call it Filmex, whose animated cartoons were used worldwide in TV commercials. Commercial cartoons are not motion pictures which have large residual values; they are only paid for once when they are made. So without its artists and execs, Filmex could not be worth much—just like that ad agency. It was now reasonably clear why the bank's executives were dejected. Here, too, the bank had no leverage, so it was plain what had just taken place.

As the elevator reached the first floor, Michelle wished fervently for a camera, but unlike stock sleuths who always carry one (or a cell phone with a camera), she had none. So she looked carefully, committing the executives' faces to memory. She saw some Filmex's executives give each other high fives as they crossed the street, and then she took the elevator back up. She downloaded Filmex's latest annual report off the company's website and scanned the executives' photographs. Sure enough, the execs had all been in the meeting: Filmex's president, its chief financial officer, corporate secretary, and two directors who were also members of the executive committee. When Michelle logged off, she stared out her window for half an hour. The world, she told me, seemed to spin around her. There was a dollar on the ground, and all she had to do was stoop and pick it up—yet, according to her PhD thesis, the dollar couldn't have been there unless it was inside information and thus criminal.

Was there anything unethical in how she found out about the restructuring? There did not seem to be.

Michelle was not an employee of the Bank of Industry, nor an employee of Filmex, nor of their lawyers or accountants or anyone else defined by the law as a company's insider. She had not bribed anyone, nor stolen any information. She had merely observed some *physical* events that took place off Filmex's premises, in a public hallway. Yet she could say with an extremely high certainty that the B of I was about to cut Filmex's debt and that Filmex's stock would in all likelihood soar as a result. Her PhD thesis said that such knowledge was not possible without inside information. Yet she was not an insider and still she had this knowledge. What was the catch?

Simply this: mathematical finance (and Michelle's index fund career) was based on *secondhand symbolic* information. But what Michelle had now obtained was *primary physical* information. Such information, *by definition*, could not be handled by math, because *it would then stop being physical*.

Michelle's career was based on the theory that the dollar could not be there, yet here was one. Should she pick it up? She came to a conclusion. She went up to her firm's trading desk (even index funds have one), and looked up options on Filmex's stock, then went back to her desk and called her broker. She told him to sell half her T-bills and all her index funds and to start buying the near-month call options on Filmex.

By the next day, Michelle had spent $15,000 buying call options on Filmex's stock—a high-risk, high-reward strategy. Two days later, when the restructuring was announced, she sold out for a profit of $90,000.

She told me all this over the latte and confided that she did not know what to do. I asked her why, and she replied that what she just did was not supposed to work, because no one could have more information than others. It was proven. "No it wasn't," I said. "All mathematical finance can prove is that no one can have more *symbolic* information than others. But *physical* information can be picked by anyone with a good pair of eyes, a strong pair of legs, and a few good brain cells." I then asked her if she was going to resign, now that her faith in index funds was shaken. "You must be joking," she said. "And give up this ringside view of free money?"

LESSONS LEARNED

What can you learn from the above example? First, that the best investment information is often *physical* evidence, not numbers or words. Not only can such physical info be important, but if you find it yourself, it could be exclusive to you, since no one has yet written about it or put it on the Internet. Therefore, always keep your eyes open for such information. Carry an electronic camera with you or, better still, a cell phone with a camera, so you can take pictures while pretending to check your calls; then e-mail the photos to your office to peruse later or to present to colleagues and advisors for identification of the dramatis personae.

Second, get to know by sight not only the independent deal makers and movers and shakers in your town (lawyers, accountants, brokers), but also internal executives like the ones above who work on restructuring, acquisitions, and other transactions that can change the value of publicly traded stocks. Seek to learn who does what in financial organizations—by name and photo—as if they were agents of an opposing power, which they are. There's no need to skulk around their offices, but if and when you see them, keep track of who they are with, follow up, and check why. It can pay off. Please note: *A lot of the physical info you'll get this way will probably be useless.* But then, so is much of the print and screen second-hand information you're flooded with on the Internet. On the other hand, when you do get a scoop via direct observation, like the one above, it could make up for any wasted time.

THE SUBJECT UNDER INVESTIGATION: PRODUCT

I n the previous three chapters, you learned how to extract people-related information by cold-reading people and their physical surroundings. In this chapter you'll learn how to extract information from the most physical item within companies, the product itself.

THE PRODUCT ITSELF VERSUS ITS NAME

P roducts can be both tangible and intangible. Microchips, potato chips, potato chip packages, pizzas, pizza boxes, furniture, and pianos are clearly tangible. On the other hand, microchip operating systems, potato chip package designs, pizza box printing designs, and music programs for organ grinders are clearly intangible. But there are also products that straddle the two categories. Books are both intangible—the book's content—and tangible—the physical book. Newspapers, broker-age reports, and soft drinks are other examples of items that straddle two categories. For example, soft drinks are often packaged lifestyles mas-querading as thirst quenchers; most sport shoes are packaged urban lifestyles masquerading as footwear.

For our purposes here, however, we'll assume that XYZ's product is solid and tangible, one that you can hold, touch, see, and take apart. The last should sometimes be done only notionally or with great caution (if the product is fragile, dangerous, or otherwise hazardous), but for the moment, let's assume it is entirely tangible. Our goal here is to unhinge your mind from "symbol-think" and to force you to *see the product physi-cally*—what German philosophers used to call the *ding-am-sich*, the thing-in-itself—not its name, its description, what a corporate public relations jockey told you to think about it, or what some analyst in a brokerage firm wrote about it.

Analyzing physical items for clues is very different from analyzing the symbols that represent them, which is what they teach at business schools and CFA programs. Indeed, in the investment world, the word *analysis* has somehow come to mean taking apart the company's financial state-ments and other theoretical aspects—corporate filings, print and Internet information, and other "reflections" of corporate physicality—leaving out the human and the tangible and the concrete. If you doubt this, take a look at the required topics for passing the chartered financial analyst exam. It is all about finance and theory and nothing at all about physical sleuthing. We've already focused on the physical aspect of commercial people. Let's hone in now on the physical aspects of commercial products.

TRANSFORMATION OF RAW MATERIALS INTO PRODUCT

For a stock sleuth, a company is a group of people doing work for other people (the customers) so that the customers will send them checks. Customers send checks because the work group sends them products or services. In the people-sleuthing part you learned to trace the physical movement of checks by honing in on the check senders. Now you are about to trace the physical movement of product by tracking its transformation from material to final gizmo, physically.

Start by assuming that XYZ makes electronic gizmos that it sells to highly skilled engineers. The gizmo buyers are all chief designers who have their own component parts budgets and who can, therefore, order parts on their own without higher approval, so long as it's from an approved list. Yes, this is unusual, but it does take place at the highest levels of tech companies. In fact, this is one of the reasons you became interested in XYZ—because its customers are worth serving. But just how does XYZ serve them? What product exactly does it sell?

To embark on the product's physical analysis, you must first get a sample of the actual product. This is a no-brainer. Yet, just as you were surprised to discover how few investors ever talk to a company's customers, you may be equally surprised to learn—or, by now, maybe not—how few investors actually examine the physical product of that same company. No, not the product's picture, its description, or its comparative place in a numerical table concocted by a brokerage analyst, accompanied by color charts. But the physical product *itself*, the item measuring 2.5 by 4.2 by 1.7 centimeters and weighing 45 grams, embossed with its serial number, cocooned within the plastic bubble wrap inside its shipment box—the thing itself.

Let us assume that you got hold of one gizmo. You have it in your hand, freshly unwrapped, still stamped with the individual identification number of the checker who tested it at XYZ's factory and pronounced it working. How did you get the product? Why, same as any customer would. Nine times out of ten, you simply call XYZ's sales department, whose telephone number you find either in the phone book or on the Internet, and order one item. If XYZ doesn't sell less than a six pack or a ten pack of gizmos, ask for a sample. Sometimes they may even send you one for free. If they balk, go ahead and buy the whole pack. Yes, it may cost you a few bucks, but it will probably cost far less than losing money on the company's shares.

What should you do while ordering the product sample? You probably know the drill by now. Chat with the salesperson and get his or her particulars. Learn about his or her job. Establish warm human contact—but not too deep and not too long here. You are calling to obtain the product, not to sleuth. You present yourself as customer, not as a money manager or investor. Still, this chat could form a basis for future contacts (something like my initial conversation with Company A's receptionist, which served as a basis for chatting with her in the fast-food joint later, as related in the Introduction). So make the phone call product-directed and reasonably brief.

I am mentioning these personal contact opportunities because unless you have been sleuthing for a while, the habit of chatting people up is probably not yet ingrained in you. Eventually it will become automatic—assimilating nonverbal cues and forming the quick nonverbal human contact, to say the right thing that will evoke a trusting response. As you gain experience, you'll find yourself getting better and better at it and doing it almost unconsciously. But until then, you should keep notes about the process: the salesperson's responses, your impressions of the salesperson's attempt to form the same kind of trusting contact with you, his or her product knowledge, attempts to sell you more ("upsell"), enthusiasm about the product, and any other facts that can give you an idea how good and committed the sales force is. Once you have placed the order, track the product's shipment time. Note whether the salesperson called to see if it arrived. Did he or she check to see whether there were any issues or problems? If there were, how well were they handled?

FIRST PURCHASE EXPERIENCE

A customer's first purchase experience is of the utmost importance for XYZ. Here is where the rubber meets the road. This is where the customer makes up his or her mind if he or she will continue to send checks in the future. If this part is botched, all the effort that XYZ invested—the hiring and training of personnel, the product design, the plant maintenance, the corporate T-shirts and morale-building picnics, the consultants imbuing employees with XYZ's culture—all will have been for naught. Because if the customer is miffed or feels neglected as a result of the first product experience, he or she will not send checks—and this would be the end of the story, the company, and the stock.

So when you place yourself in the customer's spot and buy the product, focus on all these facts, and keep notes. Not just of the salesperson's performance, but also of your reactions and impressions. These are real facts you'll use to win against those who only get their facts from the Internet and from derivatives of price squiggles.

PHYSICAL EXAMINATION OF THE PRODUCT

Let's assume that all went well and that you finally hold the product in your hand. Now observe it. You don't have to be Sherlock Holmes examining cigarette ashes to realize that physical characteristics of a key item convey important information. You can glean a lot from the gizmo's physical presence. First, you can tell whether it has been made sloppily or well, whether remnants of casting sand still stick to it or have been polished off (later you should compare it to the competitors' products), whether it is dirty or clean, whether the brochure that came with it has been printed attractively on chromo paper or on cheap tissue, and whether it reads well or has been written in broken English, whether the product is sleek or crude, looks attractive or repulsive. Yes, even in technological products aesthetics matter. Just look at Apple and its iMac, iPod, and iEverything—then see Apple's stock price.

Write down your impressions of the product, both by itself and against its competitors. Next, note how the product arrived. Was it shipped via FedEx or UPS or simply mailed? Did it get to you by name or to your general address? And if you bought it off the Internet or in a store, where was it shipped from? By examining the box, you can often see whether the product was packaged within XYZ or by an outside distributor—some packagers leave their mark on the box. Indeed, you may discover that the gizmo might actually have been produced by an outside manufacturer. In fact, many microchips (to take an example of a common tech product) are produced in Taiwan in massive fabrication lines, called fabs, costing billions of dollars. The chips themselves are designed in the United States or in Canada (that's the stage where the profit margin is highest) and then sold and marketed by various distributors. If such a product arrives quickly, it may indicate that the shipper or distributor has efficient tracking systems—or that its inventories are overflowing because few orders are placed. File this fact away for later checking. You may have hit on an advantage, or on a disadvantage, that other investors are not yet aware of. In sum, everything about the physical process can become exclusive data.

PHYSICAL ROUTE OF PRODUCT

So you are at your desk, gizmo in hand, examining it and its package for physical clues. After a while you think you've drawn as many conclusions as you can from it. What now? The time has come for a tour of the production facilities.

Assume that the gizmo was produced in XYZ's own plant—you know this because you read the corporate brochures and talked to the investor relations (IR) department. You talked to clients and suppliers and you studied the physical product, so you now call IR once again and ask to see how they do what they do and where they do it. Can you visit? Eight times out of ten, if you persist, you will get a tour. For simplicity's sake, let's assume that XYZ has one plant and one head office where the CEO, the CFO, and the R&D chief sit. It is also where the designers, the corporate cafeteria, a lab, a warehouse, and a little recreation room (where employees play Ping-Pong, pool, and darts) are located. There's also a midsized gym, which you saw in passing, with the CFO walking lazily on a treadmill and reading *Yachting World*, both of which you noted.

Once you are inside the IR representative's office, pull the product out. Point to its various parts and ask where each was made or where each production process took place. The IR person may be able to tell you or, if he or she doesn't know details, the person may bring in an engineer. This would be splendid. First, because you would then establish another contact inside XYZ, but second, you'll be able to learn the *physical* route the product goes through inside the company as it is transformed from raw material into physical product, which will later be transformed into a customer's check.

Tracking the physical conversion of raw materials into products before they are converted into checks is critical in stock sleuthing. Everything about the process here is *physical*. Before you let your sleuthing power go to your head, three specific pieces of advice are in order here and one overarching caveat.

First, the physical analysis of a product and its internal manufacturing process can be tedious and long, and one should not engage in it lightly. Nor should it be performed in great detail every time. In many cases, only the highlights of the process will suffice, since internal physical flows are best used to discover telltale physical signs that indicate *disruptions*— either a large influx of orders or a steep decline.

Second, digging into the detailed physical aspects of a product often raises suspicions in the mind of company personnel. Are you trying to ferret out their secret methods in order to hand them to a competitor? Or are you secretly working for a takeover outfit? Or perhaps you are working for a foreign government who is trying to copy their product?

If you sense such suspicions, you should address and allay them immediately, or you'll get nowhere. I have learned this from personal experience. Once I show deep interest in physical details that no other money manager has asked about, suspicions rise. This sort of questioning is not typical stock research as company personnel know it; it is more akin to operational due diligence preceding a corporate acquisition or a takeover. Therefore, I frequently have to provide references, to prove that I'm interested in the production route for stock investment, not to replicate it for a competitor. However, I do want to have the opportunity to check with suppliers regarding their ability to fulfill future requirements during high growth. At times, I've had to provide references from other companies already sleuthed, testifying that I could keep quiet about what I found, and use it only for investment purposes. At the beginning of your sleuthing career it may be harder for you to provide such references. But as you gain experience, it will get easier. But even when you start, if you are sincere, it will probably shine through your words and actions and help you allay suspicion and doubt. Moreover, in the final count, as I noted before, people do like to talk about their work; it usually takes up more than half their lives, yet very few people around them are truly interested in it, including spouses and bosses. So if you are genuinely interested in details about their work, they will tell you. Indeed, you'll often have to make them stop once they start.

The third piece of advice is addressed mainly to the engineers and techies among us. If the company you are sleuthing is a tech outfit, a plant tour may make you tingle with memories of your youth, when you built that first toy locomotive or amateur radio receiver or first small telescope. If this is the case, you may end up greedily soaking up unnecessary information and spending time on fascinating details that have little to do with key production factors. The only solution to this mind-straying is to keep reminding yourself that you are in it for the money, not just for the tech game or tech talk. As an ex-techie myself, I know it's often hard, but once you have made your first killing in a stock through sleuthing, it will become easier.

THE OVERARCHING CAVEAT

Most detailed sleuthing regarding production flow is intended to get advance information about *sudden changes* of which academic investors have not yet learned. Therefore, in most cases, this sort of sleuthing is meant for short- and mid-term trading. However, in some cases, it can also be used for finding attractive, healthy long-term businesses that are currently out of favor well before academic investors learn of their upswing. Still, in most cases, *physical product sleuthing is used mainly by traders*, and such investors rarely make real money. The serious money is nearly always made by long-term investors in terrific businesses who hold on to their positions for many years. In doing so, they postpone paying capital gains taxes, even as they get to know the terrific companies they own better and better. (This is certainly true for my firm, although it means that we sometimes hold on to good stocks even when they fluctuate wildly, because we are sure, based on physical sleuthing, that in the long term they will pay.) But just what are "terrific businesses"?

THINK LIKE A CEO WHO
HIRES THE BEST MANAGERS

Terrific businesses are those that serve worthwhile clients and are managed by smart people who decide honestly and competently how their clients are best served. If you bring this assumption to your sleuthing, you'll be thinking like a CEO who hires the best divisional managers available, and lets them run their businesses without second-guessing them, measuring them only by their results. If a CEO starts sleuthing the plants run by the divisional VPs, that CEO will, in effect, be spying on them. Even if the CEOs get good physical information through this activity, they will then be tempted to substitute their judgment for the managers' judgment. I believe this is a bad practice. Of course, CEOs should be kept up-to-date, but if a CEO should find that he or she must cultivate too many informants at a particular plant, the CEO should either change that divisional manager or sell the division because it needs so much of the CEO's own individual attention.

It is similar in sleuthing stocks. Whether a business is a terrific long-term one or not is rarely determined by sleuthing the nitty-gritty details *inside* the company. Yes, you have to do this sometimes, because, unlike a CEO, you have no say in choosing the plant managers. But you should always keep this point in mind—invest your time in the important questions, which are usually people questions, rather in the mechanical particulars, which the people you sleuth are supposed to oversee for you. In other words, track execution using sources inside the plants, but check there only for the most obvious flaws on an occasional basis, rather than reviewing the entire production process frequently.

This is not complicated, except for the part where you must stop yourself from doing things just because they are clever or because you have the skill to do them. This last part is essentially self-management, and it is perhaps more important than all the sleuthing tricks you can learn in this book. Yes, when your sleuthing skills develop, you may find yourself able to get exclusive information with great cunning and skill and then use this information to trade stocks easily. But it would be crucial to remind yourself that the one thing more important than skill is judgment, the choice regarding where to apply this skill.

Allow me to explain the importance of understanding the technical details of the product and its production. Companies are rarely ideal, and often opportunities occur when an otherwise terrific company falls on hard times temporarily. While your judgment will help you identify that company, your sleuthing skills will help you pinpoint when its stock is worth buying. And now we can go back to XYZ's plant.

STROLLING THROUGH THE PLANT
WITH YOUR EYES OPEN

Assume you persisted, cajoled, and weaseled an invitation to tour the plant. What now? What to do and say as you go through it? The ideal situation is to walk around the plant with the IR person (or your XYZ guide) product in hand, then get your guide to tell you where each gizmo's parts are fabricated, where the parts are put together, where the partially made gizmo is conveyed to be processed further, who puts it together at that next station, where it goes afterwards, which person performs the third stage, where that person sits, and, finally, who checks the finished product and where that person sits—or if the product is checked by machine, where that one is situated.

What you are after, in short, is the *physical flow* of raw materials (and raw data) through the plant as they are being worked on and transformed into something for which the customer will send checks. If the product you are after is not physical—such as software production—the process is often not dissimilar, since it also involves sequential operations by skilled people who send nontangible parts to each other, to be assembled and further worked on. Ditto for production of tangible-intangibles, such as daily newspapers, pizza box printing designs, insurance policies, and piano music rolls.

It is true that for the more advanced products or services, you may need to have a higher level of technical know-how to fully understand the conversion of data and keystrokes or machine moves into final product. But you should not start sleuthing a company unless you are able to understand the product, and there is no shame in stopping your sleuthing midway because you find that what the company does is too complex for you. Warren Buffett doesn't invest in technology for that very reason: He admits he doesn't understand it, and he's done well enough. Bill Gates, on the other hand, doesn't invest in insurance companies or newspapers (both of which Warren Buffett understands), and he's done fairly well, too. There's no shame in admitting one's limitations. The only shame, for an investor, is in losing money. So if Warren and Bill can specialize, so can you. There are plenty of companies whose operations you too can understand.

PRODUCTION BOTTLENECKS
CAN BE A SLEUTH'S GOLD MINE

W e'll therefore assume that the company you choose to sleuth is one you can understand. Still, don't invest too much mental energy in learning the entire process. Just make sure you understand it in general; then pay close attention to the parts of the process that can become bottlenecks when the company experiences a volume surge. Likewise, pay close attention to the process's parts—especially the most expensive ones, which would be the first to be shut down if the company suffers an unexpected major volume decline. Both of these cases point to where the *internal* processes can emit *physical* signals that might indicate to an *outside* sleuth that something big is happening *inside*.

I highlight "inside" and "outside" parts here, because both are matters you'll have to document diligently, since being able to receive such internal signals outside can often make you seem prescient. Just like the person sleuthing the LBO company (in Chapter 1), you may have to prove that the information you learned about that sales surge or the sudden loss of a large contract was not based on inside information but was obtained legitimately.

Documentation in the LBO sleuth's case was simply a matter of photography and note taking, and advance notification of the lawyer via a traceable device (such as e-mail). Doing the same with *physical* signals emanating from *inside* a plant or an office is trickier. The LBO sleuthing occurred in a public place. An equivalent public sleuthing would be seeing the best takeover lawyer in town lunching with the CEO of a company whose stock is cheap, where the CEO seems nervous and barely touches his food. Or seeing a company's top managers give each other high fives in the street, after meeting their bank's restructuring team. All these are physical signals emanated by insiders in public. There's no legal problem, nor even a moral one. You see the public activity, you conclude, you invest.

But what if you are after physical signals emanating from *within* the company's premises? In such a case you are no longer on public property. You are outside; they are inside. But if a signal goes from them to you, you may have some explaining to do. For our illustration, what the company does or where it conducts operations is not important. The operations can take place in an office building, where skilled employees convert data into a publication or into a software program, or in a gizmo factory, where they convert metal and silicon and liquids into microchips. What is important is the legal definition of inside and outside, and how you get the signals. If you can find legal means of gleaning internal, physical signals from outside XYZ's plant, you can sometimes find out about large changes before any symbol-investor can even dream of learning about them. Here is an example.

LARGE CHANGES IN PRODUCTION SEND PHYSICAL SIGNALS

Say, for example, that XYZ's gizmo needs to be inspected visually by an employee, then packaged by hand and signed off by that same person. During the plant tour you find that this is all done on location. The same information is available to all Wall Street or Bay Street analysts who took the same tour, but none of them, being academic investors, gave it the attention it deserves. Why?

Assume that during your plant tour you find, through delicate questioning of the IR spokesperson, that if production volume is less than 1,000 units per day, one person can do it all. What is the current level of production? You're told it's about 800 per day, which is what management told all Wall and Bay Street analysts in its guidance. In addition, management also told analysts that volume is expected to rise to about 900 units next year. This, therefore, is the production level on which all Street analysts base their revenue and profit forecast for XYZ—which is seen by everyone in possession of an Internet connection—and is, thus, the unit volume that XYZ's stock price is based on. How did XYZ's CEO (or CFO) get this information? He talked to XYZ's VP of sales, who had talked to XYZ's clients, who gave their best indications of their buying intention for the coming year.

In Chapter 2, you learned to talk to customers directly, so as to get info from them at the source rather than from XYZ—or, worse, from an analyst at a triple or quadruple remove. However, occasionally the customers themselves misjudge their future needs, because their customers have misjudged theirs. In such a case, everyone is surprised, including the VP of sales, if he hadn't kept up with XYZ's customers.

Be that as it may, the estimated next-year's volume of 900 units is what is baked into today's stock price, and that is precisely what you learn as you tour the plant. However, since your mind operates on a sleuthing level, you also ask—casually—what would happen if production rose above, say, 1,100 units per day. Yes, you readily admit, you know it now seems most unlikely. But what if it did rise to such an inconceivable level—one that had been reached only once before, at the peak of the previous cycle? Well, you are told by the guide, at such a point XYZ would need two packagers, since one would not be able to handle it all.

And, you ask absent-mindedly, where would this other person come from? Let us pause here, because as you ask this question, you must be very careful to be casual about it, because this little detail can give you, watching from the *outside*, a clear physical indication that volume has just gone up unexpectedly *inside*.

It is for this reason that you should always inquire about *physical details of ramp-up in production*. What if volume went up by 25 percent? By 50 percent? By 100 percent? Which additional machines would be needed? What extra space? How many more people? *Who* specifically would be hired? In which position? Where from? How?

The hiring needs of professional staff are often noted in a company's website, where job offers for designers, engineers, and high-level symbols manipulators, such as accountants and PR personnel, are posted. But job postings of *production* personnel—those involved with the *physical* processes—are rarely noted. This is what you are after.

FOLLOW THE PHYSICAL DETAILS

For instance, assume you've learned from the IR representative that this second packager would be the CFO's cousin. He had retired last year to serve as a part-time NASCAR crew member, but he is also available for overtime work on short notice, to complement his income and to play Ping-Pong with his old buddies. When volume surges unexpectedly, he is called in because he's available and knows the job. (And if volume rises above 1,500 units per day, his retired wife may come on board too—the job requires experience and expertise.) Now, shouldn't you mentally file both of these facts, so that the next time you phone the CFO, you can casually ask whether his cousin is still crewing for that NASCAR team that came in second place or is he working again? If you don't ask, you might be missing out on a big profit opportunity.

THE STEP FUNCTION

You asked the IR person about additional personnel needs in case of unexpected volume increase. Let us then take the opportunity to discuss production capacity and its implications. Production capacity, whether of physical items like microchips or intangibles such as software, goes up in what engineers call a *step function*. The number of machines on hand, the number of programmers on the payroll, the number of square feet of plant can accommodate only so much production volume, and no more. Yes, existing capacity can be stretched by hiring more workers and seating them in that emptied broom closet or by setting up another production machine in the company's recreation room or in the gym. But at a certain point, if you expect higher volume, you have to increase capacity by a significant amount, even though not all this extra capacity can be used immediately.

These large increases are made known to the public (and to academic investors) via press releases—plant expansions, corporate acquisitions, a new office lease. But because such information is now widely available, it has little moneymaking value left for you. Everyone learns that volume will rise, and it becomes reflected in the stock price.

EMERGENCY MEASURES SEND PHYSICAL SIGNALS

What you are after is an *unexpected* change in either demand or supply—so much so, that it has caught even management by surprise. Such changes are not announced immediately, because first they must be verified. Then, management scrambles to increase production if the surge is positive, or to cut costs if volume is about to plunge unexpectedly. Then, and only then, will management raise or lower guidance to analysts.

Hence there is an opportunity to make money before such announcements, by following physical signs that indicate such unexpected changes are about to hit.

Let's zero in on what might signal unexpected volume increases. At a time when production needs surpass the existing capacity and internal stopgap measures are employed, the CFO's retired cousin may be called back. Sleuths who focus on the physical aspects of the plant will see employees working overtime, a second shift hired, and the plant's yard filled with cars until midnight. Even a third shift, and a 4 a.m. pizza delivery. They may witness FedEx trucks parked permanently at the plant, meant to handle urgent deliveries. Signs of heightened activity become *physically visible*. You or your paid assistants stationed at the nearby coffee shop only have to watch for them, either by occasionally driving by or by watching the plant from a good vantage point.

A COMPANY FARMING OUT PRODUCTION SENDS PHYSICAL SIGNALS TOO

Another source of physical signals is one that begins with outside suppliers of peak services and products. This is because unexpected higher production can be achieved not only within XYZ's plant via extra personnel or machinery, but also outside, by farming work out to external, emergency suppliers.

Say that XYZ's gizmo needs special polishing. Usually this is done internally and up to 1,100 per day can be accommodated, according to the IR person (or the engineer who had been sent to guide you through the plant). If volume rises above that level, either XYZ must buy and install another polishing machine—which might take up to three months—or it could send the gizmo to be polished at a commercial vendor nearby. It might even send the parts to a competitor—at a higher cost per unit—but at least XYZ could then satisfy the unexpected rise in demand. How can you learn of such contingency solutions to potential bottlenecks?

The simple way to learn this information is to ask questions during your plant tour. As you meander through XYZ's plant or offices, keep asking about physical production capacity, about production extremes, and about past solutions to such situations. These questions often bring to the fore invaluable physical information about outside suppliers. What you are looking for is physical signs of a sudden ramp-up in demand—those signs that, if seen outside, are sure indications that demand has surpassed everyone's expectations, including management's. You then have to establish contact with those outside suppliers in order to learn if they had gotten extra work from XYZ.

How to do that? I'll leave this to you as an exercise in sleuthing, pointing out that the polishing establishment may have a delivery service that deals only with XYZ and the truck has a distinctive logo. Or that the polishing establishment may have a receptionist, or that it, too, may be a public company amenable to a plant tour. I'll leave the rest to your imagination.

MAKE A ROUGH PRODUCTION MAP

Finding physical clues to sudden changes via bottlenecks is often an art. But there are systematic ways to make this exercise easier in the form of a simple map. When you have a clear idea of the production process, make a rough sketch of the plant, with notes and arrows indicating how and where the raw materials and skilled labor turn into gizmos. Metal comes from the warehouse, parts come via that door over there, unloaded from a truck of Acme Supplies Ltd., and conveyed thither on a moving belt to that northwest corner of the plant, where a trio of highly skilled tool-and-die makers put the first and second parts of the doodad together. If volume rises, the CFO's retired cousin is brought in, and then he sits over there, by that southeast window, visible from that Starbucks across the road.

What if the warehouse overflows, you ask? Oh, says the IR rep, then we bring a mobile trailer to serve as a temporary warehouse and park it behind the gym over there. That gym, you see when you leave, is visible from the hill behind the elementary school that you passed on your way. So now anytime you see a mobile trailer in XYZ's yard, you know production has most likely been ramped up. You only have to go through that schoolyard and watch—or have someone local do it for you periodically. And, you ask, what if volume really breaks all records? Why, says the IR person, we would then work three shifts and have the temporary employees park their cars in that one-way street in back, whose residents already agreed to it.

What you are doing, of course, is looking for a *physical manifestation* of unexpected production volume changes.

INTANGIBLE PRODUCTION IS
HARDER TO SLEUTH

But what if XYZ produces an intangible product, such as a microchip design or mortgages or a TV program? Or what if XYZ is a large company with several plants, manufacturing many types of products and engaged in many kinds of services? When the product is nonphysical, or the company is large and diversified, physical sleuthing of the production route is often not feasible, and indeed may be near impossible, unless it aims to uncover one large key fact that you have determined to be crucial.

On the other hand, even in the case of nonphysical products, or large diversified companies, there are physical signs that can call your attention to major changes in production. And in cases where the company is of a manageable size, with a reasonably small number of facilities, it is often beneficial to start with a physical layout of the production process with a flow chart of people and material.

At the very least, it will make you think of the company in physical terms. The ideal result would be a map of the plant's layout, or even several plants or offices where the nontangible product is produced. You should know which raw material and people come from where, go where, and turn into product where. Ideally, all this should be done on a large sheet of paper with arrows and notes. Don't be put off by the difficulty or by the fact that most areas of the paper would be blank spaces. Early explorers of North America had vast patches of white spaces on their maps. But eventually, little by little, they filled the blanks with details, and they prospered. And so can you.

Once you have the product flow map, you can start tracing the external product suppliers, and the product's physical movement outside the company—where the information is often most valuable. Let me stress again that tracing the movement of product should not be taken lightly.

It is tedious and often yields little new information when production is steady. But if you are looking for discontinuities, keeping your eyes on the physical bottlenecks can alert you to things having gone awry, or gone into orbit, much before others who merely read announcements on the Internet learn of them.

PRODUCT SUPPLIERS:
MORE OMNISCIENT SIGNALS

The best physical signals of changes in XYZ's production can be obtained from those suppliers for whom XYZ represents a large or a very distinct part of their business.

Say that the company you are sleuthing sells frozen pizzas. If you find that its pizza-box supplier also supplies 50 other frozen pizza makers, all with the same kind of box, your chances of obtaining reliable, exclusive advance warning of a change in frozen pizza production from that supplier are not high. On the other hand, if you find the supplier that produces the wooden crates that the frozen pizza maker packages its product in and who represents 80 percent of the supplier's business, it would be far easier to follow that supplier's activity for a sign about the pizza maker's change of circumstances. All you'd need is to see what *physical* changes take place in that supplier's office, warehouse, and factory when its production is suddenly ramped up. Then follow up to see if these are due to that frozen pizza maker or to another customer.

Michelle's case in Chapter 3 demonstrated how tracking people who supply banking services to a company can help you foresee market changes stemming from financial discontinuity. The following example tracks a supplier of a physical raw material for the same purpose.

LIQUIDITY PREFERENCE FUNCTION

An older friend of mine, whom I'll call George, runs a midsize hedge fund. Like me, he does physical sleuthing. In some respects, I regard him as my mentor in matters of stock sleuthing. He has no MBA, no CFA, just a degree in liberal arts and a background in law enforcement. Yet in investing, I have seen few better.

One day I came to his office to take him to lunch and heard him talking over the phone. "Two kegs of champagne?" he said. "You're sure? Two?" I tried to figure out what he was talking about, but gave up as he went on, "How many bottles did you use? Thirty? Yes, I'll buy all of them, like I told you, hundred bucks a bottle. And mucho gracías!" As George leaned back, I asked him whether this was one more Silicon Valley excess. Champagne in kegs?

George didn't reply, just picked up the phone, called his broker, and placed an order to buy a large number of call options on a stock I'll call "Chiptel." I asked incredulously if he was buying stock in a spendthrift company that handed out champagne as an office perk instead of beer. "You'll lose your shirt!" George smiled and said he didn't think so. In fact, he was quite sure Chiptel would report a blowout quarterly profit tomorrow, and his options were likely to double. When I asked him how he knew, he at first refused to say, but finally relented and told me the whole story.

Chiptel was an Internet company with headquarters near Stanford University in Palo Alto. And because many Stanford business school grads want to remain in Silicon Valley, they seek jobs at local companies like Chiptel, which had no difficulty recruiting them. Those who joined, in the best tradition of touchy-feely, motivational management, brought with them the business school's custom of LPF, which is short for liquidity preference function. It is a term in economics indicating how much cash people like to keep. But in Stanford parlance, it meant the beer party thrown every Friday afternoon in the school's courtyard. A large keg of beer is wheeled in, with a carton of paper cups and, after an hour or two, tongues get loosened and MBA students get to know each other. The MBAs hired by Chiptel brought that tradition with them, but made it a monthly, not a weekly, affair. At the end of each month, when sales results were in, the company had a few kegs of beer wheeled into its cafeteria, and with everyone sipping beer, the president gave a speech urging further effort, if results were lackluster, or hearty congrats, if the results were good.

George had sleuthed another company in Silicon Valley three months before, and so got to know some local watering holes during his stay (I had provided him with a list). In one such visit to the Dutch Goose, he chatted with a Chiptel manager at the bar and learned about the company's monthly LPF custom. There was nothing remarkable about it—several other companies had imported the custom, too. However, in Chiptel's case there was a twist: George learned that when that company had an extraordinarily profitable quarter, on the evening *preceding* the earnings release day, the company served kegs of champagne instead of beer at its LPF. Where did they get champagne kegs? George asked. Why, employees of the liquor store—the same one where they got the regular beer kegs—washed an empty keg *a day before*, then poured bottles of champagne into it—maybe 15 in all per keg.

For an ordinary investor, this tidbit would have been a good anecdote to either rue Silicon Valley's excess, or to highlight motivational management practices. But for a money sleuth like George, this was pure gold, and so the first thing that crossed his mind upon hearing this detail was, "I must find that liquor store!" But how to find it? George could, of course, have asked the babbling Chiptel manager, but even though the guy was being open, he was no dummy, and so might have understood what George was after if queried directly. Instead, George just smiled, bought the babbler another beer, and changed the topic.

Early the next day, George called Chiptel's receptionist, said he was from another tech company and was planning an LPF, and asked politely where they got their beer kegs. Without the least suspicion, she told him—and even gave him the name of the store manager who was helpful to them in such matters. That same day, George drove to the liquor store on University Avenue and told the man whose name he was given that he heard they sometimes filled beer kegs with champagne. He explained that he collected empty champagne bottles, and so whenever the store did this, he, George, would buy all the empty bottles at a hundred bucks each, *if he was called right away*. I asked George, "Didn't the guy know what you wanted? Or at least suspect?" George shrugged and said that maybe the guy did or maybe he didn't. They simply agreed on the price per bottle; then George left his phone number and a few hundred dollar bills "on account."

It was this store manager who had just called, and told George that 30 empty champagne bottles had just become available an hour ago and could be picked up. Did George want them? Yes, George said, of course he did. Just have the bottles delivered to a certain address in Palo Alto. And he gave the man the address of a local friend, who would pay $100 per empty bottle upon delivery. Total cost of the transaction about $3,000. Total benefit? A high multiple of that—within two days. Because in this case, George knew with high certainty that Chiptel would report blowout numbers the next day, since the empty champagne bottles were a *physical signal* flashing from *within* the company's orbit—not from within the company's premises, but from the premises of a supplier. Like fueling truck headlights in the night preceding a missile launch, which can be seen from space, the bottles were a perfectly prescient, *physical* signal—one that academic investors would not even know existed. George had prepared the ground for this signal for nine months. When it came, it signaled a certainty. George could place a heavy bet on it, and he did. In order to enjoy similar signals in your investments, follow these four rules:

1. When talking to corporate personnel, keep your eyes and ears open to any *physical corporate habits or procedures* tied to *unexpectedly* good or bad performance.

2. Next, ponder whether these can be *legally observed from outside the company*, either directly or (as in the case above) indirectly.

3. Put plans in place to get wind of such *physical* signals. Keep doing so, because (a) only one of several such plans will yield results and (b) such results will occur only rarely. But when they do occur, they imply a near-certainty of unexpected change, and so are well worth the wait.

4. For such purposes, befriend informers wherever you can, and employ any kind of legal gratuities you can. In particular, tip generously any service provider in the vicinity of the company, so that they'll respond warmly when you call.

FOLLOWING THE PRODUCT TRAIL:
COUNTING TRUCKS AND PAVEMENT STONES

Up to now we concentrated on product movement inside the plant and in its immediate vicinity, and on movement of supplies. This sort of sleuthing, we said, is tedious and time consuming and should not be undertaken lightly. However, following the product trail *outside* the plant, though also time-consuming, is often extremely simple and can often yield exceptional results. Here is an example of such a case.

"Spencer" was a brokerage analyst who specialized in building materials. For as long as I'd known him, he was always on the verge of being fired. The reason for Spencer's precarious position was that he always gave the firm's institutional clients honest advice. But unlike other honest analysts who couched their opinions in the bureaucratic passive voice and cautious language, Spencer wrote his reports plainly and said exactly what he meant, without regard to the consequences. For this reason, he often incurred the wrath of his company's management; yet Spencer's bosses did not dare fire him, because they knew they might then lose trading business from institutional clients who loved and appreciated Spencer's straightforward analysis.

The case outlined below took place about five years into Spencer's career. It involved a midsize pavement stones manufacturer that I'll call "Bramble Stone." Spencer analyzed Bramble's financial statements, obtained information about its people and products, and prepared a detailed map of its production flow. After doing all this, he realized that something did not quite click. Either production was understated or the reported revenues were overstated. He called the company's CFO and asked for an explanation, but he was brushed off with bureaucratic jargon and complicated accounting reasoning. He checked among Bramble's competitors, but received an oddly stony silence accompanied by tongue clicks and meaningful shrugs. Spencer decided to dig deeper.

Now, contrary to what you hear about brokerage analysts, most are hard-working people who love to dig into overvalued or undervalued stocks, seeing them as puzzles. Many even get it right. The problem, though, is twofold. First, most analysts see stocks as *intellectual* puzzles—

symbolic blips on paper and screen to be decrypted. Second, even those analysts who come up with negative findings are often not allowed by their research directors to report them simply and plainly. Even if a "sell" recommendation is clearly called for, it becomes an "underperform," or at most a "reduce." Analysts accept the situation because it is the norm and because their bonuses—often hundreds of thousands of dollars per year—depend on their corporate diplomacy skills.

But not Spencer.

After doing a lot of analytical work, which included some initial physical sleuthing around Bramble's plant, he came to the definite conclusion that Bramble Stone was probably inflating its revenue numbers by including accounting items as actual sales. If this were true, the stock was not only a sell, it was also a great potential short sale. But before issuing such a scathing recommendation, Spencer had to make sure.

MAKING A FORMAL WRITTEN INQUIRY

Although all his previous communications with the company had been by phone, this time he wrote a polite letter to Bramble's CFO, with a copy to the CEO, where he asked the same question he had asked before, but more specifically. In return, he received a general rambling letter denying any problems in Bramble's reporting, urging him to pay attention to the company's "guidance" when forecasting its earnings.

At this point, most analysts would simply have dropped coverage. (Such an event is, incidentally, often a surefire signal to look into a company as a potential sleuthing target.) But not Spencer. He took two weeks off and booked a room in a motel in the small town where Bramble Stone's plant was located. (The company had only one major plant, where it made pavement stones and baked them in a large kiln and where it had its one warehouse. In that regard, Bramble was an ideal sleuthing target.)

For the following two weeks, Spencer sat in the diner across from the plant and counted the number of trucks that left the plant. He took note of all, one by one, including their time of departure. From a visit to the truck weighing station on the outskirts of town, he knew what the maximum loaded weight was for each truck and the maximum number of pavement stones that could be stacked on it. He also knew what each stone (also called a *tile*) weighed. Thus, by simple physical counting and knowing the price per tile, at the end of the two weeks Spencer found the real revenue of Bramble for that period.

When he extrapolated that revenue to the entire quarter, there was a wide discrepancy with the reported numbers. Obviously the sleuthing-time was well spent. But two weeks are not a full quarter. Spencer needed to know the quarterly revenues, yet he could not afford to be away from his office for a full 13 weeks. Even as it was, his bosses looked at him askance.

The solution was obvious. He would hire informers.

HIRING RELIABLE INFORMERS

That small town also had a university, where one of Spencer's old class-mates was now a math tutor. Spencer obtained from him the names of two reliable students who had not found summer work and hired them to sit in the same diner for the next two and a half months, counting the number of trucks. (Incidentally, he paid the students himself.) Once a week, the students also had to pass by the warehouse and see if the shelves were becoming depleted of tiles or getting filled. Thus, at the end of the summer, Spencer had a reliable estimate of the upper end of revenues for Bramble Stone.

It confirmed the conclusion he had reached before—the company could not have attained the reported sales; and this conclusion was *based on the physical count of shipments.*

Let us pause here for a moment, because the above procedure, though standard in the field of physics, chemistry, and other science—even in the area of military intelligence—is almost unheard of in the field of stock research. This may account for the trouble Spencer found himself in.

Not realizing how extraordinary his actions were, over the Christmas period Spencer wrote his report about Bramble Stone. It was no more than six pages, including a black-and-white photograph of a typical transport truck loaded with pavement tiles. It was a report unlike any other seen on Wall Street. In the report, Spencer told all institutional clients exactly what he had done, provided a table summarizing the truck trips, and offered to show anyone his (and the students') daily logs. At the report's end, based on the discrepancy between the actual *physical* product movement and the company's report, he forecasted a loss for Bramble. The company "guidance," it should be noted, had been for a hefty gain.

Before publishing the report, however, Spencer sent it to Bramble's CFO for verification, as is customary among brokerage firms. It was then that the ruckus began.

It began mildly. Spencer did not get the usual point-form comments about his research, but a short, stiff letter telling him in bureaucratic generalities that his report contained "many inaccuracies," especially to do with the accounting part, and ended in a warning not to publish such a "speculative" report.

Spencer consulted his research director, who went out on a limb and told him to go ahead and publish, so long as he was sure of his facts. Spencer went ahead and did so, and the day the report arrived on institutional clients' desks, he called them all and offered to answer questions about his sleuthing. He further told them that after the customary 48 hours lag time, in which they had time to sell the stock (as specified by the Security Commission), he was going to sell Bramble Stone's stock short in his own account, and in a large amount.

Both the report and Spencer's declared short position caused a sensation in the market for at least two obvious reasons and one nonobvious reason.

First, the report put Bramble Stone's CFO on the spot, practically calling him a cheater.

Second, it put Bramble's directors and CEO on the spot, saying, in effect, that they had no idea what really went on in their company—that they were incompetent.

But third, and less obviously, it held all *other* industrial product analysts on the Street up to ridicule, showing them up as credulous souls who merely parroted the company's line and never checked the *physical reality* behind the numbers.

THE COMPANY FIGHTS BACK

Over the next few weeks, all other industrial product analysts on the Street were invited to talk to Bramble Stone's CFO over lunch, in the company's historic boardroom. They were shown (1) industry consultants' reports proving that the pavement stone industry was healthy, (2) accounting reports confirming that Bramble Stone's accounting was perfectly in accord with Canadian accounting standards (called CICA rules), and (3) that Spencer's reports contained inaccuracies—some spelling mistakes (he was a bad speller) and also two typos regarding sales in one past quarter.

However, none of the physical claims was even addressed, nor did it occur to any other analyst to try to repeat Spencer's physical experiment and count trucks.

Let me again point out that, in any science, a question regarding the truth of a proposition is determined by repeating a physical experiment and measuring the physical results. Yet stock investment, although it is treated in universities as a science (hence the Nobel Prizes), rarely sees physical experiments such as the one above. Theories are based on symbols, and experiments are based on relationships among symbols or at most on movement of prices. No investment theory I know of is based on counting trucks, physically tracking product movement, or tailing executives.

But back to the ruckus between Bramble Stone and Spencer, which soon reached a melting point. Because by now, Bramble's stock had gone into decline, after some newspapers reported in vague terms the existence of a "bearish report" about Bramble Stone that "questioned the company's accounting."

This was astonishing to Spencer (as it was to his research director), because the report did nothing of the kind. It simply said that the reported numbers did not jibe with *physical* reality. Yet this part was not reported by any paper, perhaps because business reporters were just as blind to simple physical counting as a stock research tool as the analysts were.

OTHER ANALYSTS DEFEND THE COMPANY

By that time, several other industrial product analysts (whose firms, incidentally, underwrote brick, tile, and quarry stocks) wrote reports supportive of Bramble's position. Nearly all mentioned the numerical *accounting*, but none addressed the physical *counting*.

The stock kept sliding, so that by February, two months after Spencer's report had been issued, the stock had lost a third of its value. Now, because Bramble's board wanted to raise money by selling some treasury stock, the slide became a matter of concern for the directors, and a few asked the CFO some pointed questions.

The CFO asked the company's legal counsel to send Spencer's broker-age firm a letter, requesting formally that Spencer retract his research findings or, if not, to please stop "following" the company.

That companies make such requests is not uncommon—though they rarely publicize them. And analysts whose findings about a stock make them too bearish often prefer to drop coverage quietly instead of issuing a sell opinion on the stock, which would get them into a tussle both with the company's management and with their brokerage bosses.

Only a few years ago, a U.S. gaming analyst who had forecast that a famed real estate magnate's casino would go bankrupt was fired, following alleged strong pressure by the magnate. Not a year later the casino, indeed, went bankrupt.

No one at the brokerage firm even thought of apologizing to the poor analyst (who, by the way, is today managing money very happily).

SPENCER DROPS COVERAGE

Following Bramble's letter, Spencer's chairman told the research director to instruct Spencer to drop coverage of the stock. The research director passed the message along, but impishly allowed Spencer to send all clients a letter telling them he was dropping cov-erage under duress, at the request of the company, and he published the lawyer's letter alongside. In his parting report, Spencer reiterated his sell opinion, and cheerfully disclosed he had a large personal short position in the stock. Over lunches, he told clients that "there are always those who want to put analysts' reputation in their pocket." (Spencer was of course taking a high-risk gamble—in effect daring his bosses to fire him. But this they could not do now, since he could take them to court and win.)

At this point, newspaper reporters began to quietly call Spencer, and he informed them about the details of his research. One reporter summarized the physical part of it, and this forced the Security Commission to become involved. Its enforcement staff called Spencer, also quietly, and asked for his sleuthing notes. He let them have copies. A few weeks later, Bramble Stone's CFO, equally quietly, left for health reasons. The company took a large write-off, restated the previous year's sales, and the stock fell to a quarter of its pre-Christmas price.

Spencer's institutional clients (who ran pension funds, truly widows' and orphans' money) were saved from large losses. Spencer himself earned a handsome profit on his short position, equal to a three months' wage and larger than other analysts' bonuses. (He of course got none.) A few years later he began to manage money.

IMPORTANT LESSONS

The above example can teach you at least five lessons:

1. Count physical items wherever you can and whenever you think the result will contribute a physical piece to the puzzle, which is the company. Invest the time in this physical activity or pay others to do it for you, if you trust them to count honestly without cutting corners.

2. In order to find worthy targets for such intense activity, seek out controversy and follow it up. In most cases in the stock market, where there is smoke, there is fire.

3. In a similar way, follow up company denials and vehement accusations of analysts' "bias" or "inaccuracies."

4. Most importantly, any time you hear of a company pressing a brokerage analyst to stop covering its stock—follow up immediately! It's often a high-potential short. If you have contacts among stock analysts, ask them about such recent cases. Usually they won't

talk about them, but if you ask and promise to keep it quiet, they may tell you. Take note and follow up, because such information is potentially valuable.

5. On the other hand, *if an analyst "drops coverage" because a stock dropped a lot, it may indicate the exact opposite—a buying opportunity.* Often analysts who have been very wrong, cave in at the very bottom. If the company survives after all institutions sell its stock in disgust, based on a leading analyst's capitulation, the stock might just be worth sleuthing.

How to tell whether the analyst's cave-in is meaningful? Just look at the last pages of his stock report. In recent years, analysts have been forced to provide a stock price chart and note their historical opinions on it. Very often, you'll find that the analyst had recommended a buy at the peak, reduced it to outperform as the stock slid, then went to hold, or even underperform, as the stock had already slid substantially, and recommended a sell only at the very bottom.

Remember, however, although analysts' research can be used as pointers for which stocks to sleuth, few analysts' opinions are worth as much as a few days of direct physical observation of the company, its people, or its product movement.

COMPETING PRODUCTS—GETTING INTO THE GOSSIP CHAIN

Almost no company operates unopposed. Even Microsoft has some competition (Linux, for example). So while checking a company and its physical aspects (people, product, and plant and periphery), you'd be doing only a partial job if you did not also check the company's competition. They are both impediments to the company's success and, perhaps equally important, excellent sources of information.

In the same spirit of viewing people as the most important element of business, the first stop in investigating XYZ's competition should be the people in charge of its competitors' products or services.

How do you find these people? In the past it was often hard, but today, with the advent of the Internet, nearly every new product announcement has a name of a product manager appended to it. The name, e-mail address, and phone number appear on nearly every information release on the Internet, and product managers are often quoted in the press, sometimes with their pictures, when touting "their" products. (Most product managers in well-run companies have an incentive to do well.)

Contacting those who would know most about XYZ's competing product is therefore easy. Simply call or e-mail them.

What do you talk to them about? Same as before—say you are a money manager, interested in their product or company or industry. Ask about their product, then about their jobs—and from that point, direct the chat to the competing products. Ask about features that their own product has and that the competition's (i.e., XYZ's) lacks. Let them tell you all about the XYZ product's weakness and its failures. Or about XYZ customers who defected to their product. Or the customers whom XYZ would rather the world never knew about. Ask for these customers' names and telephone numbers.

Then call these dissatisfied XYZ customers and ask them for their experience, opinion, and, yes, job descriptions. Take notes. Then call XYZ's VP of sales and tell him or her that you have just talked to the customer who had stopped using XYZ's product and who gave you a list of the product's drawbacks. Can the VP tell you whether these defects have been corrected?

Mention in passing the advantages of the competing product as mentioned by the customer—and by the competition's salesperson.

Before long, XYZ's VP will heatedly recite to you, song and verse, the competitor's drawbacks, and customers who had defected from them to XYZ's newest doodad. Then, if you are up to it, you can go back to the competitor and ask for that person's counter-response.

If you do this delicately and diplomatically, you will learn more about the product than any analyst would. Learning about shortcomings and improvements would be especially meaningful if you take the trouble to check the product physically yourself beforehand.

What if the product is intangible? The procedure would not be much different, though there would be more focus on the product's intangible features. Ask the competitor about their product's attributes and how it compares to XYZ's. As before, call XYZ and its competitors again, follow up with loyal and disaffected customers, keep records and notes.

Once you have gone through this process once or twice (I always find it great fun), it will become like second nature to you and never again will you invest in a stock before going through such a routine. Before long, you will also start figuring out the various categories by which to compare one company's products or services to those of the competition—from the point of view of the customer and on a physical level.

THE SCENE OF THE DRAMA: PLANT AND PERIPHERY

People who make products, write checks, or talk to customers and suppliers must do it *somewhere*. This "somewhere" can be inside the company or outside, but the boundary between the two spaces often blurs. We will consider them here together as plant and periphery (P&P)—the physical environment where you sleuth for physical information. Sleuthing the P&P is most useful when a stock experiences a "negative surprise" and starts tanking. Or, worse, declines without any overt reason. At such times, as a famous market adage says, "Nasty surprises are like cockroaches." When you see one, others may soon follow. Yet occasionally stocks tank without reason, and then they soon recover. These are the best times to buy. But how can you know whether to sell the stock short or buy it up? If the decline was due to a lurking terminal problem, you may have the chance to profit by going short. But if the stock fell on unjustified fears, the decline may be the opposite—a buying opportunity.

A stock's sudden rise can nearly always be explained—a big contract, a takeover offer, a new product. But office-based investors find it hard to evaluate a stock's sudden decline. It is often accompanied by mere guesses of office-dwelling brokerage analysts, who have no clue, or by the soothing mumbles of PR jockeys.

BESTIRRING YOURSELF

Getting information in cases of a sudden decline is often harder than usual, even if you've established friendly relationships with the management team, because the CFO, the VP of sales, even midlevel personnel, will all likely be on their guard. Therefore, in such cases, the best source of information about the underlying reasons for potential disasters is often *low-level employees* who see the company's operation at its rawest, most physical level. And to get to such employees you may have to travel to production plants, transportation or distribution hubs, or even foreign lands.

Let me caution you that this isn't always easy. And, like drafting a detailed production map of a company, it is also time-consuming. But when the situation warrants it, such far-off sleuthing of P&P can bring astoundingly profitable results. Below is such a case, undertaken a few years ago by a friend of mine I'll call "Chris," who today runs a midsize hedge fund. There are several interesting lessons to be learned from this case, which I will detail later, the least of which, from my point of view, is that Chris started as one of those office-based investors who do their work solely on the basis of information gathered by others. He had an MBA degree and a CFA designation, yet he managed to shake off the "symbol-centered mindset" and sleuth his way to freedom and fortune. And if he could, so can you.

A HUGE DEPOSIT IN A FAR-OFF PLACE

Chris was then a twenty-eight-year-old analyst working for a Canadian bank's pension fund, as assistant to the VP of pension investments, tracking the stocks in the pension fund's portfolio.

On the day in question, a mining stock held by the bank's pension fund began to sink. The year before, that mining company had discovered a huge platinum deposit in a country I'll call Freezonia situated in, shall we say, central Asia.

Platinum is not as well known as gold, but it is used widely both in industry to clean up emissions in cars, for example, and in jewelry. Platinum is more expensive than its yellow cousin, so the lucky find made waves worldwide, and the mining company's stock, let's call it "Z-Plat," rose from fifty cents to fifty bucks, at which point it became respectable and well known enough to be included in the market index. So the pension VP bought it.

The day the stock began to sink, the pension VP called Chris and asked what was going on. Chris didn't know, but said he'd check. He called the brokers who had raised money for the company and now followed the stock, but none had a clue, nor did Z-Plat's VP of finance nor its chairman, both of whom Chris also called. That night Chris scanned the Dow Jones, Reuters, and Bloomberg services, as well as the Internet, but none had anything about Z-Plat. The next morning, however, the mystery was partially solved—the mining company issued a press release stating that its geologist had had a fatal accident falling off a suspension bridge, but that his assistant had been promoted and operations were proceeding as planned. There was no need for alarm. Brokers immediately sent e-mails to their clients, saying the recent decline was excessive and should be seen as a buying opportunity. The stock rose a tad, but then it continued to sink.

NO ONE KNOWS ANYTHING

Was anything else going on? No one seemed to know. So the bank's pension fund VP asked Chris to perform a thorough analysis of the stock. To do that he would compute its financial ratios, profit margins, income forecasts, beta correlations with the market—just as he had been taught in his MBA program and later as part of the CFA program (which he had to pass to get his Chartered Financial Analyst designation).

All afternoon Chris busied himself at his computer, doing ratios and graphs and forecasts, working from brokerage reports. Everything looked good—all the ratios were healthy. But the stock kept sinking. So, contrary to all he'd been taught, that night Chris called the main branch of the Freezonian National Bank in Freezone-Town, half a world away. (Why the bank? Because banks usually know the local score, went Chris's reasoning.) When the branch manager heard Chris's question, he rudely hung up. Chris suppressed his annoyance and called the Canadian embassy in FZT and asked to speak to the commercial attaché. But that man snapped that he knew nothing about stocks and could not comment. The commercial attaché at the American embassy, whom Chris called next, also could not comment. And the French commercial attaché, whom Chris called also, merely laughed and hung up the phone, as did the editor of the English-language newspaper in FZT. That did it for Chris. By two in the morning, angry and discouraged and hoarse from shouting into the long-distance crackle, he went to bed and slept badly. He did not know yet that he had just embarked on the road to fortune.

CURIOSITY IS THE MOTHER OF ALL SLEUTHING

Next morning, with the French attaché's laughter still ringing in his ears, Chris's anger slowly turned to curiosity. What did the locals know that no one in North America did? He thought about it, and finally called his boss and told him he'd have to go to the library to collect more material for the spreadsheets, and so might be away from the office for a few days. The VP agreed, and it is here that the story turns instructive. Because instead of going to the library, Chris went to his bank and withdrew $9,900 in cash, then called Freezonia Airlines and booked an open two-way ticket to FZT, charging the $3,540 to his credit card. That afternoon, dressed in jeans and carrying his knapsack, passport, and a Freezonian map printed off the Internet, he took a cab to the airport.

Now, let's pause here, since you may be asking why Chris didn't tell his boss where he was going. Why did he pay for the trip himself? There were three reasons. First, Chris knew the bank's VP would never go for such esoteric research. Research was done on paper and by reading brokers' reports, not by flying to faraway places where one had no contacts. Second, the bank's pension consultants were wedded to the Nobel Prize–winning finance theory which says that all information is in the market already, and thus trying to beat the market is futile. One simply has to diversify by buying all the stocks in the market's index, while still keeping a prudent eye on them, according to the theory. But the third point is that, perhaps in his inner heart, Chris recognized an opportunity when he stumbled on one, though he didn't know it yet.

IF THE BUTLER DID IT THEN THE CABBIE KNOWS

The flight took 17 hours, during most of which Chris slept. When he landed at FZT airport, he drank a large coffee, and for $250 in cash hired a cab to take him straight to the Z-Plat mine, which was 120 miles away. During the trip, Chris struck up a warm conversation with the cab driver and learned much about the local business climate. For example, he learned that the president's son was a silent partner in most local busi- nesses, as well as in the platinum mine. And that there were family rela- tions between the president, FZT's chief of police, and some generals, all of whom were investors in the mine. This was widely known throughout Freezonia, but not in North America, apparently.

Three hours after he landed, Chris arrived at the small Freezonian town where the mine was located, at the foot of rocky hills. The town was little more than shacks on stilts built around a dirty main street with three bars, one café, and one general store. Chris paid the driver his $250 and added a $100 bonus, asking him to wait. He spied half a dozen locals dressed in coveralls waiting at the roadside café, so he sat down to chat with them. Chris learned they were mine workers, helping to construct the smelter. When he asked if he could visit the mine, he was told that the mine was on a rocky hilltop with access only via a suspension bridge crossed by a military truck, which would be arriving soon. It would bring one shift out and take the waiting workers in. Chris sat tight. He was nine thousand miles from his office and there was no Z-Plat analyst or broker in sight, but he felt like he was making progress.

SCHMOOZE-Y DOES IT

As Chris waited, he struck up a conversation with the mine workers, asking about their families and their work. They were happy to tell him about the former, but reluctant to speak of the latter. Chris did not press them; instead he handed out cookies he had brought with him from Canada and told the workers some bawdy jokes. Two locals who spoke English translated, to great hilarity. At last, to reciprocate, some local guy told Chris funny stuff in return.

"The geologist who fell off the bridge? Heard about him?"

"Well, yes," Chris said cautiously. "What about him?"

"Well, he had two wives and nine children, and to keep them all happy he had to work triple duty. But lately he had enough and said he wanted to quit."

"Enough of what?" asked Chris. "Of keeping the two wives satisfied?"

At this there were giggles, but no answer.

Chris went on, "And when he couldn't get away from the wives he jumped off the bridge?"

One worker laughed. "Yeah, sure, jumped. With a boot mark in his butt."

Chris asked, "Maybe one of the wives got mad and hired the boot-wearer?"

The hilarity became tinged with nervousness. "Wife? None would dare. Not for a man working for the president's son."

Chris waited, but there was no more. Because he himself began to feel nervous, to make conversation he asked about the new geologist. Was he good?

At this there was raucous laughter. "The geologist? Who needs a geologist? The president's son sends people at night to paint the rocks to improve their color before sending samples to the lab. See?"

"So what are you doing here?" asked Chris.

"Building a smelter for visitors to see."

Just then the truck arrived. "Do you want to see the mine?" someone asked. But suddenly Chris did not feel like seeing the mine. As a matter of fact, suddenly he did not feel too good at all. Here he was, thousands of miles from home, near where geologists who might have been about to squeal about platinum-mining scams fell off suspension bridges with alleged boot marks in their butts. The word "risk" suddenly acquired a deeper, nonacademic meaning, having little to do with beta correlations. Chris thanked the workers, handed them the rest of his cookies, shook awake the snoozing cabbie, paid him $250 extra to drive back to FZT, and promised to throw in a hefty bonus for speed.

All the way back, Chris kept looking over his shoulder, half expecting some military jeep to chase him. But he arrived in FZT without mishap and that same night flew back to Toronto, via Mumbai, Qatar, and London. He landed Friday morning, slept 15 hours and said nothing to anyone about where he had been or what he had learned. Absolutely nothing, to anyone. And this, please note, was just as extraordinary as his initiative and, in fact, marked him as a successful fortune-gatherer.

MEANWHILE, BACK IN CIVILIZATION

Monday morning Chris came to the office, still said nothing to anyone, and put up the entire bank's stock position in the mine for sale. Sold it a dollar down and then went to the VP's office to tell him of the sale. The Veep asked angrily why this was done without consulting him. Chris apologized and showed his boss some old spreadsheets and spoke of highly negative beta correlations and other MBA claptrap. Since Z-Plat's stock was by that time five dollars down, the VP accepted it, and even commended Chris on his good statistical work.

Back in his own office, Chris called his lawyer, told him the story succinctly, and asked if he was clear. The lawyer said it was probably okay, since Chris had not stolen anything, had not trespassed on company property, nor had he received any official information from the company's executives. All he had was gossip and innuendo. Wasn't it? Chris said this was indeed the case, absolutely. He thanked his lawyer, and sent an e-mail to his boss, telling him he might buy a put on Z-Plat's stock in his own account, now that the bank was out. The boss e-mailed back that Chris should keep in mind that unlike the purchase of respectable large stocks where risk could be quantified, buying puts was risky and speculative. But it was Chris's money to do with as he pleased.

Chris thanked the VP for the advice, promised to be prudent, and next called his own broker and sold half the index funds in his self-managed retirement fund and bought short-term puts on the mining stock. (A *put* is the right to sell a stock to someone else at a specified price before a certain date. If the stock falls quickly, you can make several times your money.

If it rises, or even stays flat for a while, you can lose all your money.) The following day, Chris withdrew half his remaining cash savings and bought more puts on Z-Plat in his regular trading account. He had still told no one of his trip, except his lawyer. Not his parents, his friends, or his softball buddies. He acted, after taking legal advice, and kept quiet.

By the end of four weeks, Z-Plat had fallen from $45 to $20, and Chris's puts, which he kept adding to, had ballooned in value to a quarter million dollars as the stock fell. By then some rumors began circulating about doubtful rock samples, and the stock plunged to $12 in one day and then jumped back to $15 when latecomer short sellers were forced to cover their shorts and were squeezed out. Chris doubled up on his position, putting most of his profits at so-called risk. When the stock fell to $5, he doubled up yet again, and yet again at $3. When two weeks later the stock fell to $0.50, he closed his entire position and took a day off.

A month later, Z-Plat went to zero. It was found that the mine had been salted with platinum dust floated in acetone, which was sprayed on the rock samples before these were sent to the lab to be tested, to make the mine seem richer than it was. And how rich was it? What was it really worth?

MYSTERY REVEALED: THE KING IS NAKED

In a word, zero. Nada. There was no platinum. The strongman's son and a few generals had bought a lot of stock in a defunct Freezonian mine, folded it into a public company on the Canadian stock exchange, and presumably paid the polygamist geologist to "salt" the rock samples with platinum dust to boost the share price. When the geologist (who had a lot to live for) got cold feet and thought of copping a plea to the authorities, who, of course, told the strongman's son about it, he suddenly and fortuitously fell off the bridge, and the locals dumped their remaining stock position on the market. This was what had caused the stock to plunge initially. Whether Z-Plat's chairman and finance VP were in on the geologist's death was not known. As for the strongman's son, he is now before a Freezonian tribunal stacked with his father's cousins, so his future may not be so grim. But certainly it has been grim for pension funds and other runners of "other people's money." Collectively, they lost about $2.5 billion.

And Chris? He made 1.9 million dollars in six weeks. A month later he resigned and rented a small office in downtown Toronto, at the foot of Bay Street, with a good view of the lake and within walking distance of the health club. Today he manages his own money and that of some close friends.

THE HOLY TRINITY OF INVESTMENT CRITERIA

Chris's sleuthing philosophy and principles are very similar to mine. The principles include what I call the holy trinity of investment information, which every sleuth must always keep in mind—investment information is valuable only if it's *true, important,* and *exclusive*. If any one of these crucial three components is missing, your money is in danger. Here is why:

TRUE VERSUS MISLEADING: If the information isn't true, it's not information; it's disinformation, put out by those who act for and get paid by the seller, such as PR flacks, or stockbrokers who want to sell a slug of stocks for insiders.

IMPORTANT VERSUS IRRELEVANT: If the information is not important, you shouldn't care how true it is. Such information would include statistical fluctuations of the stock price, expressed in math—which is as relevant to the company's value as the statistical variations of the number of cranial hairs of its board members. In both cases, you can get exact statistics that would be absolutely true. But so what? It's as if you were trying to gauge the value of a novel by counting its word frequency. (But see Appendix B for just such a theory, developed along the lines of efficient market theory.) Indeed, brokers' reports are full of irrelevant data arrayed in graphs and charts that are a waste of your time.

How can you decide whether some data is relevant or not? There are no shortcuts here. To figure this out you must develop a reasonable understanding of the industry—and this means talking to people who participate in it and getting to know what's important.

Warren Buffett once said he knows of a man who made a fortune in water utilities because his expertise let him compute the exact impact of each flush of a toilet in North America on earnings per share of each of the water utility stocks. Such expertise might be a bit too detailed for your purposes. All you need to succeed is to know more than the index fund investors, which is next to nothing, about the hundreds of stocks they invest in. If you learn a reasonable amount, you will already be far ahead.

EXCLUSIVE VERSUS KNOWN TO ALL: The information must be exclusive to you, because even if what you learn is both true and important, if it's not exclusive to you, then the stock price probably already reflects the information. Therefore, by definition, information you read in corporate filings or over the Internet or in the paper, even if it's true and important, cannot make you much money. Yes, you can lose money if you are ignorant of it. But you can't make much money using public information only—you need to sleuth for exclusive information yourself.

What if one component of the holy trinity is missing? The answer is do nothing. Stay in cash. My money management firm may keep a cash component for months on end, until something comes up in which we can get an exclusive edge. As Warren Buffett says, the biggest sin is to lose money. The next biggest sin is to tie up your money in mediocre investments, then not have enough for the really big score, when you have exclusive information.

As you saw in Chris's example, one of the best ways to get exclusive information is to talk to workers low on the company's ladder. In Freezonia, Chris learned about the platinum-salting scam from the lowliest mine workers, the diggers and the simple construction crew. They all knew what went on. What about midlevel personnel—the kind who, for most sleuthing, are the best source of information? Not in a case like this. With a scam, the persons you should resist talking to are the midlevel supervisors. Although they probably know more than the crew, they are already a rung up on the corporate ladder and want to climb higher still, so they won't tell you much, and might even report your interest to the scamming bosses. So if you want to know something when sleuthing a scam, ask the rank and file. They know the true facts, and if you talk to them straightforwardly, they'll very often talk to you the same way. And what they know is often both true and exclusive.

But would low-level employees understand enough of the larger operation to discern what's important and what isn't? Actually, the men and women who run production lines and make offices run smoothly, who perform low-level customer support and sales functions, who design products and fix them when they are faulty, know more than one would imagine. More often than not, they do the real work while the top brass plays with spreadsheets. Indeed, low- and midlevel employees are among the smartest and most capable people in any company, and often know more than the bosses realize. What's even more important, low- and midlevel employees rarely have a financial cushion, often living from paycheck to paycheck, and therefore have to keep well informed about the company's fortune. They talk to Gladys in purchasing, to know whether the plant has ordered more parts or less, they chat with Sam in sales, to learn whether more or fewer orders are likely to come in, and they check with Jeff in product returns, to learn whether the new product has been accepted by the customers with enthusiasm or returned with rude comments.

Getting information from such employees, Chris tells me, is often like money in the bank. He only has to talk to them to learn the important truth about a company—and this knowledge would likely be exclusive to him. And in case you are wondering why they would talk to you, let me repeat what I noted before. In my experience, low- and midlevel workers often know much more about their company than their bosses, yet many bosses rarely talk to the worker-bees, and even more rarely do they listen to them. Yet everyone likes to be listened to, so if you just ask the workers questions with genuine interest, it's likely that they'll tell you whatever you want to know. You only have to listen, and you'll be amazed at what you'll hear.

I asked Chris what else was important. He said that once you found something exclusive and important, you must learn to keep mum about it. It may sound obvious, but it's among the hardest things to do.

FOCUS ON WHAT YOU KNOW

Before you ask, no, you don't have to fly to faraway and dangerous places to get exclusive, triple-good information. There are probably publicly traded companies in your own town, whose operations you can learn and whose people you can talk to. If you apply yourself to the task, you can very likely learn more about these companies than any analyst or faraway money manager. Do your work well, and you'll take these academics' money, as Chris and I do.

And to repeat for the umpteenth time the most important lesson, and perhaps the hardest, when you finally find out the important information that no one else knows, keep your mouth closed and buy (or short) quietly.

RADIO DAYS: GETTING EXCLUSIVE TIPS IN PUBLIC

To obtain exclusive information, as I've said, you should aim to get close to the company's customers and learn exclusive facts about them. Public information is usually only of marginal value. Yet once in a while, it is possible to get exclusive information from a public source. If this seems like a contradiction, please recall the New York sleuth described in Chapter 1 who received valuable information from a magazine about the catering habits of the LBO firm. Yes, his follow-up was not something that ordinary office-dwelling investors would consider, but it did flow from a publicly available fact.

Thus, even though public information can give you very little advantage, every now and then a publicly stated fact can be a starting point for fruitful sleuthing—if you follow up properly. Let me share an example from my own experience. In this instance I received exclusive tradable information over the radio, from a public interview.

SLEUTHING HIGH SOCIETY

I was visiting Waterloo, Canada's minor Silicon Valley. I had come for a poker game with two former business school buddies now working for a wireless device company and to gather gossip about who was doing what to whom in Waterloo's tech-land. Gossip is an important part of money sleuthing, and I fully expected to get some from my poker friends. But this time, surprisingly, I got the exclusive information from public radio.

I was driving up to the restaurant to meet my buddies for dinner, where, upstairs, we would later play serious poker, drink Chevas, and smoke Cohibas. It was 6:30 p.m. and I turned on the radio, searching for a jazz station. Instead, I got a daily interview program on a popular radio station. I heard the interviewer speaking with "Clarence," a famous Toronto fashion designer, and nearly twiddled the dial onwards, when I heard Clarence mention the coming Technology Charity Ball, for which local Waterloo women would be buying exclusive apparel. I had been to the ball the year before, accompanying an informant, and was interested to hear any gossip about it, so I cocked an ear.

The interviewer asked, "And who would you be designing a dress for this year?" As usual, Clarence would be making only one dress for the ball, and for this exclusivity he would charge a hefty price. "Ah," Clarence said. "This time it's for Francoise Chipper." I raised the volume. Francoise was the wife of a software entrepreneur genius, an ex-Englishman I'll call Edwin Chipper. Edwin ran the eponymous Chipper Software (a.k.a. Chipperware), whose up and down fortunes could put a Ferris wheel to shame. He was also a carefree rascal who was rumored to park his Jag anyplace he desired, and to collect parking tickets, ladies' phone numbers, and occasional shiners from enraged boyfriends and husbands. But the previous year he finally married a lovely local esthetician of French-Canadian ancestry, Francoise, whose passion for couture made her Waterloo's most renowned fashion plate. I had seen her photos in Chipperware's annual report, where she was a director. Francoise's picture also appeared often in the local newspapers' fashion pages, wearing her latest wrap, which she helped design. Francoise considered herself both a fashion icon and a cultural role model for local dowdies. (They saw it somewhat differently.) It was clear that her appearance at the Technology Charity Ball would be followed closely.

"And what dress will Francoise be wearing?" the radio interviewer asked breathily. Clarence explained that, unlike last year when Francoise had worn a mauve toga lamé, this year her costume would be future-oriented. And, Clarence added, he had been authorized to disclose what it would be. The interviewer pressed him to reveal the secret.

GOSSIP REVEALS EXCLUSIVE INFO

There was a dramatic pause. "A black velvet bodysuit with matching knee-high boots, each elegantly embedded with a precious stone at the knee area," Clarence declared at last. "A joint design by both of us." For which design, he added nonchalantly, a matching pair of twenty-carat rubies had been ordered and would next month be flown in specially from Tiffany's office in Caracas. "For how much?" the interviewer asked. "Oh, about $1.25 million," said Clarence. "Each. Give or take." I nearly drove off the road. $1.25 million? $2.5 million total? How could poor Edwin pay for this? His company had been losing money for two years!

The interviewer apparently had the same doubt, and wondered whether Francoise could afford such a garment. "Isn't her husband's company in, er, difficulties?" Clarence chortled, "That's what I thought. I told Francie that Tiffany would require cash in advance. And you know what she said? 'No problem,' she said to me. 'Next month Edwin could easily pay for two pair.'"

I took a deep breath and brought the car to a full stop at the roadside as the radio interview ended with catty chit-chat about frumpy dresses cobbled by Clarence's competitors. But I no longer listened. I sat blinking into a vista of financial possibilities. Did the wife of a madcap entrepreneur just tell the world, via her exclusive designer, that her hubby's company, of which she was a director, was about to earn at least $5 million next month? I eventually restarted the car and continued on my way to my poker buddies.

CONFIRMATION IS CRUCIAL

Later, during the poker game, I steered the chat toward Edwin Chipper. How was he doing? Was he indeed going bankrupt? Well, maybe he was and maybe he wasn't, said one of my buddies, but he had heard that a few engineers in Chipperware were buying shares; next month their purchases would probably hit the Insiders' Buying report. Why were they buying? My buddy shrugged. He had heard their new wireless circuit was sort of cool, although he personally didn't think it so great. Yet, evidently, Chipper's engineers thought differently. Or maybe they were just mesmerized by their boss, who could charm the skin off a starving cat, my buddy said. I nodded. Buying by insiders could be misguided if insiders followed a charismatic boss, as my own experience showed. Still, more often than not, insider buying was spot on, so further verification might be called for.

In the poker game that evening I lost $150 because I was unable to concentrate. Later that night I tossed and turned in my bed at the local Holiday Inn, unable to sleep, and by morning I resolved to check it out. After breakfast I drove to the coffee shop across from Chipperware's headquarters, where I had several coffees and sat listening in to the engineers talk. They were too far away to hear clearly, but I caught a few snatches about travel and sales presentations, nothing informative, yet the tone was excited and happy. I returned to the hotel and phoned Edwin Chipper himself.

I had met him at the previous year's Tech Charity Ball and had kept in touch, so he took my call. I told him that I and a few partners were looking to make investments in local wireless companies whose prospects we liked. We had heard he was having cash problems, but under some conditions we might buy newly issued shares directly from the company. Was he interested? Edwin laughed heartily in posh. "At these prices? No bloody way!" Matter of fact, he said, he had wanted to buy more new shares himself from the company, but the board wouldn't let him. "Not at these prices and not with the prospects. Anyway, wait a month, then we'll talk." He cheeri-ohed me and hung up.

Edwin's seemingly careless revelation of wishing to buy shares and good prospects might have been mere promotion. He was very talented this way, and more than once got into trouble in such matters. But refusing outright an investor wishing to give him cash? Edwin had never refused cash before; he was always in need of more. I felt my heart accelerate. Was Francoise's designer right? Were her ruby-decorated boots illuminating a buying opportunity? Or was it mere boast?

During the drive back to Toronto I pondered the question of how to check the designer's comment. Finally, an idea struck. Chipperware owed $9 million to a U.S. wireless company I'll call "Ether," following the acquisition of one of its subsidiaries. The debt was supposed to be paid in quarterly installments. Who then would be better placed to know of Chipperware's true situation than its creditors? Like the bank who holds your mortgage, and which keeps track of your employment situation, to make sure you can pay up, corporate creditors also keep track of their debtors' situation, to make sure their debt is safe. That same afternoon I called Ether's headquarters in Massachusetts, said I was an institutional investor, and got to speak to the assistant treasurer. After some queries about their balance sheet, I asked whether they had any fear that Chipperware would not be able to pay the debt installment coming up in a few weeks. My worry, I said, was about Ether taking a loss on their loan.

"What loss?" said the lady. "They already paid, three weeks in advance." When I expressed unfeigned surprise, the treasurer said indifferently that Chipperware's new wireless circuit apparently had lots of advance orders, most with prepaid contracts, and so they had lots of cash to redeem their debt to Ether early. "You should have no fear investing in *our* stock," she said. I thanked her warmly, hung up, and called my broker.

What happened to the Chipperware stock, you ask? It went up more than sixfold. We caught only about fourfold of this, because (as usual) we sold too soon. However, our too-soon sale proved fortuitous, because when the stock was riding highest, Chipperware acquired a revenueless bubble, centered on a nonexistent market, and in a few months the stock plunged back to where we had bought it. And before you ask, no, we were not smart enough to short it at the top. There was no radio interview with Francoise by that time, nor with her designer.

YOU ONLY HAVE TO KEEP YOUR EARS OPEN

Yes, getting exclusive tips in public is rare, but not unheard of. If you keep your ears open, you may get such exclusive info more often than you might think. Here are a few possible scenarios:

Say that you know of an important XYZ conference to which XYZ's most important customers are invited to give their opinions about the product and suggest improvements. There have been rumors about coming defections by some important customers, which, if true, would indicate that the product is unsuccessful, with major implications for the coming year's revenues.

In the company's annual meeting you are introduced to the wife of one of XYZ's key customers. You had learned (from the investor relations rep) that this customer has been slated to make the keynote speech in the conference the following Saturday. During your chat with the customer's wife, you learn that the coming weekend she and all her family are about to go camping in Yellowstone. What about the conference? You ask. "Oh, that," she says. "I don't think Bob will be going." This piece of information, I am sure you realize, is in the category of triple good—important, true, and exclusive. It is now up to you to devise a strategy to find out whether Bob's company indeed intends to drop XYZ's product.

Here is another scenario. You are chatting with the cousin of XYZ's CFO, whom you met earlier, and asking him about the coming month's NASCAR race. Will he be in the pit? Oh, says the CFO's cousin, maybe not, he thinks he might be needed at the plant. This info, too, might be in the category of triple good, if you remember the earlier information about expanding capacity in case of sudden large contracts.

I could provide more examples, but there really is no need. Once you develop the sleuthing instinct, you'll find yourself listening for clues and hints about internal goings on in the company whose stock you covet. Don't be surprised to get such clues even through newspapers, radio, or TV. But you do have to follow up to confirm or refute the clues. This, like all sleuthing, is work, but it can be very enjoyable too.

CHAPTER 6

WHODUNIT:
PUTTING IT
ALL TOGETHER

The many parts, tricks, and techniques of sleuthing can be displayed most effectively in a format called a *Starmap*. A Starmap has two main advantages. First, by letting you display all the information comprehensively, it can provide a focus for your helpers (if you have any), who can view each other's work, discuss it, and draw conclusions. Second, the totality of the display often leads to an "aha!" experience when disparate elements suddenly mesh. The Starmap often helps you see where the stock is about to go.

The Starmap technique presents the company as a network of social relations among its employees, customers, suppliers, competitors, bankers, accountants, and other important peripherals, with the final result looking like a starry constellation. Lines drawn between individuals, according to their social connections and past associations, where they live, what they do, who they are married to—indeed, all information your sleuthing team could obtain—create the star shape.

As an aside, the Starmap is a much-reduced version of what intelligence services create when they want to visualize the internal relationships among members of the opposing team, or what police departments do when they want to trace connections among various organized crime families. Kremlinologists, too, used to draw such maps to gain an understanding of where various members of the old Soviet *"nomenklatura"* (important members of the party) stood in the informal decision-making structure.

THE REAL WORLD REVEALED

Starmaps reveal what really goes on in the world, physically and socially, as opposed to what is being reported in the press or in corporate filings. So although making such a map is not a trivial undertaking (if you aim to produce a comprehensive one), even a partial Starmap with only the primary players drawn in is often enough to give you insight into how the company really works, as well as who is doing what to whom and why.

The one clear case when a comprehensive Starmap is nearly always called for is when you or your team want to get a handle on a future event, such as a merger or a takeover, and are searching for ideas about physical items worth sleuthing. In such a case, where you are embarking on a pending event investigation, a Starmap is a necessary ingredient of the situation room, where the focused investigation is centered.

The Starmap came out of my preferred mode of sleuthing, which involves making lists of those who might know what I am after, or who might know those who might know it, and then phoning around to get references and introductions, until I hit pay dirt. As you can see, the telephone is my preferred sleuthing tool. (That and beer.) As I've said before, others have a talent for making people confide in them in person, but my own peculiar skill is to have them tell me things on the phone. My first choice is often to call those insiders who have been buying stock, say that I am a money manager, and ask them the reason for their purchases. Often the simple question, "Why have you been buying?" if asked with admiration, elicits a detailed response. But market regulations have taught executives to be cagey, and properly so. This is why I began keeping detailed lists of nonexecutive members of a company's personnel, or its suppliers, and eventually the lists ballooned until they became the Starmap.

DEGREES OF SEPARATION—AND CONNECTION

Here's how you can make a Starmap of your own. Start by taping two or four large paper sheets together and spread them on the floor or on a large table. Draw a circle in the middle and write in it the name of the company you are sleuthing. You must now view this circle as a hub of physical and social human relations, with as much past history as possible. The relations are internal and external, formal and informal, new and old. Soon enough you'll see which ones are relevant; but start by putting in as many as you can.

Then, draw smaller circles around the company's name and, inside these, write the names of key company personnel: executives, key designers and engineers, salespeople, directors, major shareholders who influence strategy—anyone you think is an important part of the ongoing human drama inside.

Now, for each circled name, write his or her age, education and work history, ownership of stock, work function, and any other data that connects him or her to the company. If you have the person's picture, wonderful, glue it on.

Next, mark down addresses and background information, as much as you have. If you can, put the addresses on a map, and glue the map at the corner of the Starmap. Note on the map any major social hubs for the company, such as a golf club where all executives play, bowling alleys where engineers go once a week, a restaurant where salesmen meet to schmooze, and so on. The details depend on your diligence, the importance of the deal, the amount you think you can invest—and on the amount you think you can gain. (I told you sleuthing is often hard work.)

If you do this diligently, you'll soon begin to see some clear patterns emerging. This executive was in high school with that one, the VP of sales lives on the same street as the CFO and the chief designer, but the R&D chief lives on a mountaintop at the edge of town. Is it important?

You don't know yet, but it's something you keep in mind. Or, when you look at the personal histories, you see that this person was in the Army with that other person, and so on. You don't want to overdo this social connections part, because first, corporate people often do what they must based on the company's needs; and second, corporate people move, and doing too much work on some personnel who may be gone tomorrow may be a waste of time. But the top people often stick around, so learn as much as you can about them—yet not too much, because we are only starting.

Next, draw balloons around the company, inside of which you'll write the names of the major customers—corporations, distributors, or any organization that buys what the company sells.

FOLLOW DA MONEY, METICULOUSLY

Next (you guessed it), note the names of the individuals in these organizations who (1) vet the product, (2) use it, and (3) sign the checks that become XYZ's revenues. Note as much information about these important check senders as you can. This is crucial, since it is the beginning of "following the money." Getting the names of these individuals and details about them is often the most difficult part of the sleuthing process. But you must do your best to get it since it is key, as we've seen before.

At this stage, you'll again begin to see patterns emerge—patterns of where the money flows, from whom to whom, and maybe the first inklings of why. You may see that this main customer's buyer went to college with that designer, or this customer goes to the same sailing club as XYZ's VP of finance, or this check sender is married to this salesman's sister and even lives on the same street.

The more information you have about the company's people and its customers' people who are in touch with them during the sales process (or the after-sales process), the better. This is the bedrock on which commercial relations are based. Now draw lines that show the connections between the company's people and the customers' people. Social, familial, historical, living areas, hobbies, or any other you deem important. Write notes to yourself (I find sticky notes useful here) regarding what you should check further.

Now do the same for the main suppliers, bankers, accountants, and so on. (If you have a team, have others do this in parallel to save time.) As you progress, further patterns will begin to emerge—who knows whom, who spends time with whom, who had been together with whom in the past, where and when, etc. This is the physical reality of the company, describing the real relations the company's people have in the commercial world in which they live.

Last but not least, now add further balloons in the margins of your large sheet, and write in the names of the main competitors, their main personnel, and perhaps their main suppliers and advisors.

THE LIVING COMMERCIAL ORGANISM

The entire process can be lengthy, and it should not be undertaken for small investments. But if you've managed to get this far, you'll now acquire an understanding of the word *company* that index fund investors or academic investors will never have. You'll begin to see the company as an organism that lives both among its friends and among its opponents, inside the community and alongside, where people have a multiplicity of relationships—some during work hours, others outside work, still others dating from years ago, with common associations, memories, and experiences. In short, you'll begin to see the company as a human drama in progress, with main players and supporting cast, with a past and a present, and through these you'll now try to see the company's future.

Finally, to bring the drama into sharp relief, draw lines signifying social connections among the various people on your large sheet. Use different colors to show different connections. For example, you can use pale green to show people who went to college together and so have a similar social background, and dark green for those who went to the same school the same year and so probably know each other personally. You can use pale blue to show those who worked together before elsewhere—for example, at IBM—and so probably have the same corporate habits and outlook. You can use dark blue for those who worked in the same department at IBM at the same time and so probably know each other well. Add colors to indicate those who have the same hobby (if you can find such information), those who engage in the same sports, those whose sons or daughters go to the same schools and who therefore probably meet each other during school functions. Don't forget those who are related to each other by marriage or those who used to be and no longer are. You are probably wondering what possible use you could have for all this.

WHO IS THE POTENTIAL BUYER?

Well, assume you are sleuthing a company whose stock is extremely cheap. You have heard rumors from midlevel personnel in the industry, whom you have plied with my second-best sleuthing tool, that a larger company in a similar business has been rumored to be eyeing XYZ as a takeover target.

You'd love to know which company this is, because then you can sleuth its people, or pay students to stand in the lobby of the company's office building and wait for its VP of corporate development to emerge and see which strangers he is walking with. If one of these is XYZ's CFO, you may have hit pay dirt. But how to find out which potential acquirers might be stalking XYZ?

Well, it is true that some acquisitions and takeovers are born in the fertile mind of Wall Street or Bay Street financiers who present ideas to corporate chiefs. But the majority of acquisitions are done by companies who have some personal or social contact with people of the acquired company, and these acquisitions go more smoothly.

Therefore, for a first guess of who might be the potential stalker of XYZ, take a look at the past-work-history colored line on your Starmap. You'll see which personnel used to work together, in which company, and when. Of course you'll have to sleuth for confirmations—or refutations—but the social Starmap could provide you with an excellent starting point.

SLICK NEW RIVAL ON THE BLOCK

The Starmap is also an excellent visual aid for discovering potential competitive threats to a company whose stock you own.

Assume that your Starmap shows that the check-signing buyers at XYZ's main customer have all attended Stanford business school, same as XYZ's sales VP, and all are members of the local car-racing club, while the top salesman of XYZ's competitor has come from that Other Biz School in the East, and he is a skeet shooter. XYZ's competitor has been doing badly, perhaps because its product was not as good or perhaps because of a bad fit between its top salesperson and its customers' buyers.

Now, assume that one day you read in the *Wall Street Journal* that XYZ's competitor had fired its VP of sales and hired another, whose name is given. Out of curiosity, you sleuth the new guy's background and realize that, unlike his predecessor, he, too, is a Stanford business school guy. What's more, his father had been a famous car racer, and he, too, raced during his sophomore year. So you pick up your Starmap and color the line leading from XYZ's main customer's buyers to XYZ's competitor a deep red, to show both the same background and the same hobby.

Is this information relevant? Of course it is, because the risk of XYZ losing customers to its refurbished competitor has just gone up. It is a risk that the market may not yet perceive; certainly index fund investors won't see it, because they are blind to the human element of investing. But you, with your Starmap, would see the connection.

You naturally still have to confirm or refute your finding. How? By calling XYZ's customers. During your chat, ask them casually about the new VP of sales at XYZ's competitor. What's he like? Is he a good guy? If you then hear a bubbly enthusiasm about the new man, and if you happen to own a lot of XYZ stock, you may conclude that further sleuthing is in order—or perhaps even some trimming of your position because XYZ's stock's future may not be as rosy as before.

This sleuthing trick, like most others in this book, is very simple. But it requires having visual information at your fingertips. Unless you are a compulsive note taker, or have a photographic memory, the Starmap can be an excellent aid here. And if you have others helping you with your sleuthing, these others can refer to the same data, discuss it, and either add to it or delete the parts found to be untrue or irrelevant (so long as they leave notes about who changed what when).

PHYSICAL SURVEILLANCE

If you also plan visual surveillance of the plant and premises, the Starmap can be a useful visual aid. Consider adding to it photos of the plant or the warehouse—or even photos of the same at the customers' premises, just to concentrate on the physicality of your work. Lastly, if you add a map of the transportation route between the company and its main customers, you would be laying the ground for finding possible locations for physical sleuthing later, should the need arise.

I already mentioned that you can glue photos of the company's key personnel to the main Starmap for easy reference. Equally useful would be photos of the main customers' buyers and of the company's bankers, lawyers, accountants, and other advisors, provided you can get them. If you are sleuthing for an "extraordinary event," such as a merger, an emergency financing, a restructuring, or the like, such photos will prove helpful.

THE SITUATION ROOM

When the Starmap begins to bulk up with information, usually it is because it is needed for a specific project. Then you'd better start thinking about a situation room or war room. You often see these spaces on TV programs featuring police detectives who are looking for a killer or who are trying to guess where a serial killer on the loose will strike next. If you are trying to find out about a large contract a company might get, a takeover or a merger, or any other extraordinary event, the Starmap could be enhanced if you use it within a situation room.

Such a space is simply a dedicated area—preferably a room that you can lock—where you can hang up your Starmap, tack photos on the walls, put up clippings from magazines about the company, its competitors, clients, or business, as well as photos of the plant. You could even post a photo of the Starbucks across the road, with the plant-facing window circled, to show your team where they can go to watch the comings and goings.

In other words, when the situation warrants it—when the deal is big enough and important enough—the situation room could resemble a homicide department squad room during a crime scene investigation (CSI). The same holds true for an intelligence service, when it receives a tip of a pending event that it would like to prevent. Its people would then perform a similar procedure, drawing maps of potential locations, making lists of involved persons, drawing line connections between people with common interests, and hanging the map up in a secure situation room, where the team can refer to the map and update it.

The difference between a CSI and a pending event investigation is that the first tries to find out what happened, while the second tries to find out what's being planned and is likely to happen. Your type of investigation would most likely resemble a pending event investigation more than a crime scene, but in both cases, having all the data in front of you and your team would help tremendously. A Starmap can help focus your efforts and enable each member to benefit from the findings of others. (Not least is the benefit of knowing the background of each person you call, as you call him, so that you can talk about things dear to his or her heart—such as fishing, or car racing, or the military.)

The technique is effective but also time-consuming. Furthermore, it takes you away from other stocks you may be following, so one cautionary word is in order here.

Since using a Starmap is an advanced sleuthing technique, I suggest you not try it full-scale immediately. Leave it for after you've managed to gather some experience. But you can—and should—use parts of it, to focus on the information you gather about a company, its people, customers, and peripherals. Starmaps help get you in the sleuth's frame of mind very quickly by helping you spot all the connections, obvious and hidden.

TIPS AND BENEFITS

Here are some tips for using Starmaps to get the greatest benefit:

1. Treat stock analysis not as a special branch of bookkeeping, but as a police investigation of sorts regarding a pending future event.

Learn as much as you can about all the actors involved, who they are, what are their motivations, skills, personal and professional details—everything. Doing the task thoroughly is very tedious, but when done well, it will help yield significant results.

2. Whenever you sleuth an especially promising stock, where the outcome of a future event is in doubt, set aside a situation room at your home or office, just as police and intelligence agencies do, with a whiteboard, wallboards on which to tack maps and photos, and a list of tasks to be done. Make sure you and your team can see all of these when you make your phone calls.

3. Draw a Starmap with the relevant connections among the main actors: company, clients, competitors, lawyers, accountants, bankers, suppliers, etc. Take special note of past workplaces, hobbies, birthplaces, families, community involvement, affiliations, declared ambitions, and—often most important—other people's opinions about each participant. This topological social Starmap is the human reality—who knows whom, who talks to whom, who likes (and dislikes) whom, who does what to whom, and why. (That's one of the things that efficient market theory misses, of course, because these things aren't expressible in math.) Hang the Starmap prominently in the situation room.

4. Once your brain is filled with a critical mass of physical details and social connections related to the stock you are sleuthing, the drama will come alive for you soon enough. You may even get weird hunches; follow them. It's similar to the hunches actors get about a character in method acting: Once they learn enough details about the character's background, he or she "comes alive" for them.

Conversely, if, in the midst of an investigation, following all your accumulating knowledge, you get a strong intuitive feeling there's no deal here, disengage and go to another stock. Giving up time spent is easier than giving up money.

NOTE OF CAUTION

If you use Starmaps to follow social and family connections of all involved parties, you will likely learn a lot of sensitive personal information. *Treat this information with respect.* Lock it up securely in the situation room and *never talk about it.* People have a right to their privacy, just as you have a right to yours. If you don't abuse confidences, you'll get more of them in the future.

PICKING STOCKS TO SLEUTH

M any books offer advice on how to pick stocks, so I'll limit my advice to picking stocks to sleuth—that is, how to narrow the large number of publicly traded stocks to a very small list, where physical sleuthing has a higher probability of finding bargains. The very definition of bargain, of course, denotes a cheap stock—either in relation to its value now, which everyone else ignores, or in relation to its future value. It may be currently undervalued either because the business is better than what most assume (which is the kind of stocks that Warren Buffett likes to buy) or because its future growth will be stronger and last longer than most appreciate.

I call the four categories of stocks cheapies, goodies, rockets, and tradies.

1. **CHEAPIES** are value stocks of the kind Ben Graham recommended—stocks trading below book value, below working capital, at a low PE, at low cash-flow multiples, with a high dividend yield, and so on. These are also the stocks that Warren Buffett began his career with—cheap values. You can find lists of them in any ValueLine survey of stocks that you can get at your local library.

2. **GOODIES** are stocks of excellent businesses with a lasting franchise that keep generating earnings and growth even with mediocre managers. Buffett's partner, Charlie Munger, has always been a fan of such stocks. It was he who recommended them to Warren Buffett, who saw their merit and changed his investment style. Munger recommended buying franchise stocks even if they are not very cheap, because their ongoing value creation will make them cheap eventually. So if such goodies tank temporarily because of some transitory problem, so much the better.

3. **ROCKETS** are momentum stocks. These are stocks of companies that experience explosive growth, such as Microsoft, Cisco, Dell, or Taser, all in their heyday. If you buy them even at a high price and hang on so long as they grow, you can make several multiples of your money. Or you can lose it all if you don't get out in time, which is what happened to most investors in the tech bubble stocks after 2000.

4. **TRADIES** are a sort of catchall investment category that covers special situations, where a sharp change is about to take place. If you find out about this change in advance, you can buy the stock from (or sell it short to) those who don't know about the change.

Which category is best? There is no clear answer. Every investor has a personal bias toward the kind of stocks he or she feels most comfortable with, and you have to find yours. Which is mine? Both my money management firm and I have a strong bias toward a combo of the first two styles: stocks of good technology businesses that unjustifiably became temporarily cheap. We call such stocks *value techs*. When we find such stocks, we sleuth the heck out of them, and if they are found worthy, we buy and hold them until they (hopefully) become rockets. At that point we sell them to the momentum guys, who kindly take the risk of weakening growth off our hands.

WHY STOCKS GO TO THE DOGHOUSE

S tocks become values for many reasons, but tech stocks fall into the value category for only a few reasons. The first and foremost reason is a product crossover: This is a situation in which an old product is dying and the new product that is supposed to supplant it does not yet sell at a similar volume. This occurs even as the heavier capital investment and R&D spending depress earnings or cause a loss. At such times, you can often pick up good tech companies for a song, if your sleuthing finds that the product crossover is proceeding normally and is about to succeed.

Or, a tech stock can fall into the value category because its particular market niche is now in a cyclical trough. And just as everyone thought the stock was going to the moon when it peaked, now they all think it is going to zero.

Well, some tech stocks do go to zero, but only rarely in the case of stocks of tech businesses producing crucial products or services for the tech economy, as you'll see below. How to find out if this stock is safe? You guessed it—sleuth it out.

Other times, there may have been a temporary mess-up in a good company, which new management is now trying to turn around. For example, a company "stuffed the channels." This means they sent out to their distributors more product than they knew could be sold, but booked it as revenues anyway. This makes growth appear that isn't truly there and boosts the stock artificially. Oddly (or perhaps not), such errors usually occur before management exercises stock options and sells stock. When such shenanigans are found out (they almost always are), the stock tanks, management is often kicked out, and the board brings in professional consultants to put systems in place to ensure that such chicanery never happens again.

Or management may accord itself backdated options (deciding which back date they'd price their options at). It's like betting on the roulette in

Vegas after the wheel has stopped turning, and you already know where the ball landed. Such actions are reported in accounting mumbo jumbo in the annual report, but this, too, is nearly always caught; then the stock tanks, the board turfs management, and brings consultants in to fix the problem.

You get the idea.

The upshot is there are several types of corporate shenanigans which negatively impact stock prices and which, at first glance, look terrible to the uninitiated, but in fact are easy to solve. And once they are solved, they create a stronger company with stronger systems that will prevent future shenanigans for a year or two, create a more attentive board, and bring in new management who are often better and watch their step.

FOR A SLEUTH, TEMPORARY PROBLEMS ARE MONEY IN DISGUISE

I love these kinds of problems. When I find them, and my sleuthing shows that the problems are being fixed, it's often an opportunity to buy a good company which is becoming even better, at a cheaper price. My own field of stock hunting is technology, but you may choose another—banking, oil and gas, mining, real estate—whatever field you have expertise in. But no matter which sector you choose, it'll no doubt have stocks suffering from temporary problems, where fixing has already begun but where the stock price does not yet reflect it.

How to find stocks suffering from temporary problems which you can sleuth out? Read the papers. Peruse the Internet. Look for the dramatic stories, for the shenanigans, for the cheating, for the fraud. But please also note that this is not for the faint of heart, because in some cases stocks suffering from what you may think are temporary issues, may really be in the throes of a death spiral and are ripe for shorting. Yet if you do your sleuthing properly and don't cut corners, you'll soon discover which case it is.

How do I find such companies? I already mentioned that my own bias is for value tech—tech stocks that fall into the value category. As a first screening, I look for *neglect*, *cheapness*, and *reemerging growth*. If you look for these three characteristics, you can't go far wrong no matter which industry you concentrate on. (But you must remember that this is only the first step, not the last. It is only the precursor to sleuthing out the real story.)

Let me show you how the above three qualities matter.

NEGLECT

Neglect is usually the result of stocks that had been rockets in the past and disappointed egregiously, or were run by rascal managers who messed up, or, indeed, any stock that has fallen from fame and glory into blame and so-sorry. When a high-flying stock crashes and burns, those who still own it are often so ashamed that they simply try to forget about the stock. Often they don't even sell it at a loss. Such stocks end up tucked away in corners of IRAs, private accounts of brokers (who often get mesmerized by their own stories), or institutional portfolios, such as mutual funds or pension funds, where they are legacies of money managers that have been fired. In the last case in particular, such disgraced stocks are not known by the new managers who have been brought in to fix the mess. And— this is key—such new fund managers usually have what is called the *30 days' grace* period—a month during which they can clean up the portfolio they inherited and sell the disgraced manager's stock picks *without regard to price*.

If you now know more about the disgraced stock than the manager who is selling it, you can buy a value stock for a bargain price. It is not hard to do if you find the right stock and if you dedicate sleuthing time to it, because when everyone else actively shuns a stock, even a little bit of real knowledge can go a long way.

I must caution you here that neglect by itself is not sufficient. Many neglected stocks deserve to be neglected, but not all. Therefore, the second criteria we look for is cheapness.

CHEAPNESS

How do you know if a stock is cheap? There are about a gazillion and a half books about how to find cheap stocks, starting with Graham and Dodd's bible for value investors and ending with many modern ones. The value metrics are either the general ones noted above, or they can be industry specific. You can seek moderate value, which means only so-so cheap, in which case you'd have more stocks to look at, or you can go for deep value, which means dead-cheap bargains, in which case you'd have far fewer. Warren Buffett, for example, used to buy net-net stocks—those that sell below net working capital (working capital less all liabilities), essentially buying the company for less than the value of the minerals in its corporate body. If you want to look for such stocks, ValueLine Investment Survey will provide you with lists. (When the market is cheap, you can find a page full of them. When the market is expensive, you may find only two or three or even none.)

By the way, the equivalent of net-net stock in the tech world is called a *walking wallet* (WW), a tech stock trading at less than its net cash. You can find it only once in a blue moon, and when you do, you can be sure that the stock is suffering from an extreme aversion by its shareholders due to past management screw-ups, overoptimistic analysts who have now turned superpessimistic, and, most likely, a cash bleed that looks as if it may soon drain the company and lead it to bankruptcy.

It is that last quality that gives such stocks their name—they are like perambulating wallets with a hole in the back trickling out cash at a rate that indicates they will run out in a few quarters—you can even compute how soon this would take place.

Again, as with other cheap stocks that deserve to be so, some walking wallets, too, deserve their insultingly low price, because some do indeed stop walking and die cashless, eventually. But not all. Because sometimes management of such bargain stocks realizes there are no tooth fairies in the market and gets a grip on the operations, cuts costs, and stops the bleeding. Or at least they stem the bleeding and indicate it will stop in X quarters. When such bold action takes place, the WW can often take off, for at least two reasons.

First, when the WW stops hemorrhaging cash, it proves the business is no longer a mere hobby, may be a viable one, and is worth more than the mere cash per share.

Second, other companies may have cast covetous glances at the WW, wishing to acquire it, but waiting until the WW's management runs out of cash and then comes crawling to ask for a deal. If and when the WW's cash bleed begins to taper off, such an acquirer must suddenly scramble to offer a buyout, because the WW will soon no longer be desperate. And if there has been more than one potential acquirer, a bidding war may even break out.

Based on my experience, a WW whose bleeding is being stemmed can often zoom 50 or 100 percent above the cash value. So if you manage to find such a stock, sleuth the cost-cutting efforts and the integrity of management. If you find both satisfactory, only then (contrary to the normal order) sleuth out the clients, because if the first two are lacking, the clients may not be worth much, since the business could be closed. But if everything comes out roses, the stock may be worthwhile.

The term *walking wallet* was actually coined jointly by me and another sleuth investor, a friend of mine who runs a hedge fund. Both he and I ended up buying for our funds a package of 10 WWs. And we both sold the packages a year later, for a stupid gain of 35 percent. Why stupid? Because of the 10 stocks, only one went belly up, and even that one distributed half the cash to shareholders. Of the other nine, two went up threefold, and one went up fivefold. How come? Their businesses were far better than we had suspected. In retrospect, it would have been worthwhile to sleuth out the WW businesses better, but hindsight is always 20/20.

If you find a WW and your sleuthing shows it to be a worthwhile buy, don't sell it before you sleuth its business thoroughly, because you may just miss a multibagger.

REEMERGING GROWTH

Besides neglect and cheapness, growth is what you are after, or else you can simply buy a stable business cheaply for a one-time gain—like Warren Buffett's three-puff cigar butts. But even if you aim to catch an awakening growth stock, you must keep in mind that growth does not always appear immediately. My own bias is toward neglect and cheapness, but only in cases where we think we can get growth (I hate losing money). Then we hold the stock as long as we can—I also hate paying taxes, and capital gains are lower than gains on short-term trading. For this reason, we spend time sleuthing stocks with potential long-term advantages, rather than short-term nifty trades.

Over time this method works out fine. But I must warn you—if you use such a method, you'll occasionally have to wait a year or two before the exclusive info you've found filters down to the public at large. Thus, your portfolio may stay flat for a year, or even two, before the stocks wake up. But when they do, they often make up for the long wait, as does the lower tax rate you pay on the eventual gain.

Now how do you look for growth? First, the usual way. Talk to the customers, who should be happy; to the competitors, who should be nervous and surly; and to the suppliers, who, like the customers, should be happy. Indeed, when a company is on the rebound, its suppliers may often be a better investment. But this, too, you can find out when you go out and sleuth it.

There is also a second way to find where growth may be coming from—by following where both the company and its customers have been focusing their time and money. If you hear that the company has been hiring R&D people for a certain technology, and the customers have been hiring people experienced in using the very same technology, you may glimpse the future when it is still in the intention stage. Training schedules are also a great predictor for a customer's intentions, as is spending to house potential users of future purchased products. But no matter how you sleuth it, look for growth—and aim to buy it as cheaply as you can.

HOW TO FIND SLEUTH-WORTHY STOCKS

Searches can be divided into text searches, database screens, and gossip.

TEXT SCREENS

If you look for stocks to short, search for any combination of words that indicates a brewing disaster or a problem. Such word combinations could include "Management denies that…," "left (resigned) for health reasons," "left to pursue other interests," "lowered guidance to…," "reiterated that the rumors have no basis…," "filed a lawsuit against short sellers…," "VP of sales/marketing left for personal reasons…," "company hired a new VP of sales…," "management took issue with the analyst's conclusion…." These word combinations indicate an insufficiency of sales not yet announced, messed-up financial statements not yet admitted, or otherwise show management is sticking its metaphorical finger in the corporate dike to prevent damaging information from leaking out. The limit to what you search for is bounded only by your imagination.

You can either Google terms online, or if you or your broker has access to a Bloomberg terminal or news service, you can also search either of these for the word combination you have an interest in. They will give you all the news items or public information releases that emanate from companies where affairs are sticky and are likely to get stickier.

Similarly, you can simply go over the morning newspaper with the same mindset, seeking brewing disasters. In general, a good sleuth has a dirty mind and a clean heart. The dirty mind helps him see the self-serving reasons behind most commercial pronouncements, but his clean heart prevents him from holding this against the pronouncers. Most are merely trying to take your money, just as you're trying to take theirs.

If you are looking for long tradies, you may screen for words that indicate that a perceived disaster is not as severe as others think. Such word combinations might include "debt reduction surpassed…," "cash grew faster than…," "settled a lawsuit…," "sold the plant/real estate/division…,"or any such statements that in your past sleuthing proved significant. These are signs of subtle improvements (signs of deploying capital more profitably).

Here, too, the limit to what you can look for is bounded only by your creativity. And yet again, once you find what you are looking for, the work is just beginning. This is when you start sleuthing.

NUMERICAL SEARCHES

Text searches are really searches for companies that conform to an idea you have about what a company would say when things begin to go wrong or go right. But the same can be done through database searches, if you have access to them. The best searches rely on the simple but powerful idea of supply and demand balance or imbalance.

You can look for scarcity of supply about to meet rising demand and buy the companies who would benefit; conversely, you can seek too much supply where demand is drying up and short the overextended companies that would be hurt.

How to find such imbalances? Jimmy Rogers, whom I consider to be one of the best fundamental investors, and an occasional sleuth, once explained in his conversation with Jack Schwager (in one of the early *Market Wizard* books) that he looks for industries where capital spending does not even equal depreciation. That is, where everyone is so depressed and demoralized and sure that bad times are here to stay, they don't even spend enough to keep plant and equipment in good working order. This was the steel industry in the 1990s, the nuclear industry after Three Mile Island, and the oil and gas industry when *The Economist* magazine famously came up with a cover story about the "glut of oil." The cases are many.

To find such industries, start by looking at the most depressed ones, then do some research work about capital investment versus depreciation. If you find sufficient signs of industry depression, browse through filings, do some ratios, and if they prove rust has been spreading through an industry's productive capacity (metaphorical or otherwise), start talking to industry insiders to gather physical evidence of your conclusion—this, as always, is key.

If you (or your broker) have access to a commercial database such as Standard & Poor's Compustat®, you can screen for whatever criteria you desire. (The following is meant for those with such access. If you don't have it, you can skip the following few paragraphs.) For example, you can look for all industries (either by GIC or SIC code) where the sum of last three years' CAPX (capital expenditures) is smaller than the sum of DP. Or you may look for the industries where PPENT (net property plant and equipment) has fallen two or three years in a row (meaning that capex is less than depreciation) or any other item that signifies productive capacity in that industry. If you have made yourself into an expert in that industry, you'll know which item that is. It would vary for different industries.

How then do you match this with a rising demand? Be creative. You can, for example, look for accelerating growth in sales (SALE/SALE[-1]-1) or for a rise in sales in relation to inventories—SALES/INVT—meaning that sales growth has outpaced management's forecasts, who hadn't stocked up

enough inventory to satisfy burgeoning demand. Or, you may look for growing gross margins (GM), showing a stronger pricing power on the part of
the companies in the industry, or for any other parameters you can cre-
atively think of. When signs of stronger demand occur in an industry where
total production capacity has been falling, you can be sure you may find a
few stocks where sleuthing would be more than worthwhile.

Remember, playing with databases will not give you profit. This is just
preliminary work to direct your real work. What will make you money is
shutting down the screen and either picking up the phone to call that
industry's participants—customers, suppliers, management, and employees—or getting out of the office altogether and going to sleuth out what
really goes on in the seemingly depressed industry, where things may just
be waking up. The screens and databases are just pointers, a sort of radar,
to start you off in the right direction, nothing more.

PERIODIC (CYCLICAL) DISASTERS

Many businesses are cyclical. Some cycles depend on the economy—
the housing market, for example, or the cement business, the steel business, the metals business. Other industries have a cycle of their own: for
example, the microchip business, where every three years a new genera-
tion of microchip is being made, with ever-finer resolution.

If you follow a specific cyclical industry and become an expert in it,
just buying its stocks at the bottom of the cycle and hanging on to them
in order to sell them close to the top would make you a wealthy person in
only a few years.

But how can you know when stocks of a certain industry are close to
the bottom, and when they are close to the top? And how can sleuthing
help you find out?

Let me give you an example from a field in which Giraffe Capital has
some expertise, microchips. Say you investigated the industry, talked to
engineers and other insiders, read the literature, and concluded, as we
have, that the making of microchips is a complicated activity divided
into six or seven stages, each of which is so complex that it has only one
or two companies with a dominant or semidominant position. The production stages are easy to define. First, you melt the silicon, then cut it

into slabs, polish the slabs, impregnate them with ions and other impurities, cover the slabs with chemicals, project photo-masks on these, etch out the circuits, etc. Each of these stages is crucial for the final microchip to be made, and most of these must be performed in absolutely clean rooms, some of which are also emptied of air to a very high degree.

In other words, it is an industry where only experts can participate. But once an expert company has established a large market share in its segment, such a company is hard to dislodge. The price for this secure position is a breathtaking roller-coaster ride with the microchip cycle—with plunging sales and often losses at the bottom. But the prize is soaring sales and mouthwatering profits at the top.

Which companies should we sleuth here? That's easy. When we talk to industry contacts, we can ask them which company they admire most in each of the manufacturing stages. Which would they like to own, if they had the option?

Usually only the very best names come up. These companies, if the industry were not cyclical, would always be expensive, so sleuthing them would be a waste of time, unless we waited for a one-off (noncyclical) screw-up. But because the microchip business (indeed the entire technology business) is very cyclical, we are in luck. Once every three years or so, various companies that help produce microchips—those that make machinery to cut, chop, polish, etc., or those that make the clean rooms in which the microchips are made—can see sales rise 50 percent in one year or lose 50 percent of their sales in the next. This is next to perfect, if your aim is to make good gains without tying up your money in the company for too long, while still paying lower capital gains taxes. In the two- to three-year period between cycles, stocks can double and triple or be halved and quartered. It's up to you to find out which. You already know how—in any industry you wish.

GOSSIP, THE PROFITABLE GRAPEVINE

After playing with databases and other seemingly sophisticated methods, talking about gossip almost seems like a letdown. It shouldn't be. Although seeking industry gossip seems a fuzzy method, often it is the best means of finding out what really goes on in the commercial world.

All you have to do is chat with industry participants, ask about who does what to whom, then keep your mouth shut and your ears open, and listen hard. If you can do that, you'll find that people tell you the most amazing corporate secrets—who is about to be fired, hired, or sired, as well as who won, who lost, and who is leaving to take advantage of an opportunity that industry outsiders have not yet glommed onto. You may hear detailed complaints about products not fulfilling expectations or about other products surpassing expectations to such an extent that the buyers are buying them in bulk for their offices nationwide. You may hear about lawsuits, accounting gimmicks, stuffed channels, or SEC queries that may soon become full investigations.

Where can you get such info? Why, the same place where you do your sleuthing. Wherever members of your target industry congregate, schmooze, bowl, or unwind. Once you get into the real gossip flow, you may have an edge that stay-at-home and academic investors don't. Use it to your advantage.

CHAPTER 8

SLEUTHING BLOOPERS—TWO CAUTIONARY TALES

T he risk in the powerful stock sleuthing methods is that you can get an inflated head, which can lead you to make mistakes and lose money. It has happened to me more than once. In cases where I knew more about the company than anyone else, I imagined I knew everything. It was at those times that ignorance of simple public facts tripped me—as it can trip you, if you are not careful. Therefore, and to balance the nifty sleuthing techniques you learned in the previous chapters, I thought it prudent to tell of two painful anecdotes from my own experience in which I lost money despite textbook sleuthing. The fault lay with an inflated sense of my own ability.

I hope you pay close attention to this, because once you start using sleuthing techniques, and you are also lucky enough (or unlucky enough) to make a long string of profits, the risk of an inflated head is a very real one. What I would urge you, then, is to cultivate a sense of modesty and balance, even as you become better as a sleuth.

The first anecdote highlights the dangers of knowing nearly everything physical about a company, its customers, and its people, yet neglecting two simple matters: reading the corporate filings in detail and recognizing a faulty business strategy.

SUPERFAST COMPUTER INC.

One of my first bloopers involved a midsize tech company in Silicon Valley, which I'll call Superfast Computer Inc., or SCI for short. I found it by browsing though our databases, and via some informants in Silicon Valley. (Most of our picks come through several information channels simultaneously.) I was surprised to see that the stock was as cheap as it was, because the company was a technological marvel—and it still is, even after filing recently for bankruptcy.

At the time, SCI made, and still makes, some of the best supercomputers in the world. These computers can perform zillions of operations per second, can power aircraft simulators, compute the effects of atomic blasts, plot the path of hurricanes, and help design rockets. Indeed, some of SCI's computers were so fast that there really were very few competitors who could take clients away from them. Sure, the less sophisticated computer companies kept nibbling away at some of the marginal functions that SCI's machines handled, but SCI reigned supreme as the monarch of supercomputers, and its clients loved it ardently. I know, because I talked to dozens of them. Only later did I realize that such excessive happiness by customers is often not a sign of strength. Indeed, it may be a sign of weakness, because the company may be doing the customers a favor by serving the very specialized top of a market, where it could keep its position only by spending more and more, within a market niche that could not expand (since lower-end competitors were constantly increasing their capabilities).

Clients should not be ecstatic, they should only be happy. Thus, being at the very top of the technological heap is also not an advantage, because the company may again be doing its customers a favor by doing what no one else can do or bothers to do. Being able to only grow upwards, by

spending more and more money on R&D in a static niche, is a silly strategy, especially since the lower end of the market is being eaten away by
lower-end competitors. But this I only understood later.

At any rate, once I stumbled on the stock and saw how cheap it was, I
began to research it. I made a list of the company's main customers and
called about a dozen of them, while my assistant called a dozen more. We
called the competitors, too. We called company personnel in two foreign
subsidiaries and customers in foreign air forces, universities, and research
centers all over the world. Everything looked wonderful. And through it
all, the CEO kept buying shares for millions of dollars. After a while, his
top lieutenants bought, too. I traveled to the company's headquarters in
Silicon Valley, got myself invited to its campus, and met its personnel. A
happier, smarter bunch I never saw. They ran around the place on communal blue bicycles, chatted with each other amiably, and often were
seen accompanying customers, who were also happy.

Everything looked good. The stock was cheap. Was anything wrong?
Well, there was one little flaw. The company had some debt, in the form
of convertible debentures. Nothing unmanageable, or so I thought, certainly not with so many customers in their pocket, not with such a superb
brand name, not with such wonderful technology. So after a while we
began to buy—at around $3 a share. The stock rose to 3¼, then slid back
and fell below $3. We bought a bit more. It kept sliding. We checked with
customers. Everything was fine. Well, there were some revenue timing
issues—some orders may be delayed to the next quarter, but nothing
severe, not with such a cheap stock. (We thought.)

Then one order was delayed, the company missed its revenues forecast,
and the stock dropped to $2. Because of our risk controls, we sold. Then
we checked. What did we find? The loan covenants for the convertible
bonds specified rigorous cash flow and revenue "coverage ratios." When
the revenue was missed, these levels were broken. Normally the bank
holding the debt relaxes the covenants in exchange for another quarter
or half a percent of interest. Not in this case. What we didn't realize (we
were so busy sleuthing the company that we didn't check who owned the
bonds) was that a small portion of the debt was now held by an aggressive
U.S. hedge fund, and that fund refused to go along with the relaxation-

refinancing unless it received some warrants for the refinancing. In other words, it wanted a portion of the company.

The company would, of course, have to give the same deal to all the bondholders. Suddenly these bonds became more valuable, because it was clear that the company's value would go to them, not the stockholders. It was then, when we were almost completely out of the stock, that I received a phone call from SCI's investor relations guy. He wondered politely whether I would be willing to exchange my bonds for the new kind of bonds the company was proposing, with only a moderate amount of warrants attached—that is, with a small portion of the company's value as a sweetener. The company offered only a stingy sweetener because its chief now owned lots of stock and didn't want to dilute it. Normally this is a worthwhile sentiment, but not at times like this, when the task is to get the deal done and move on.

When I heard the IR rep's question, I realized two things. First, that he thought I owned bonds, which I didn't, and so, like me, he didn't have a good handle on who owned them. But second, the attempt to refinance was going badly, so the bondholders were likely holding out for more of the company's value. This meant that the stock was probably going down further. Perhaps a lot further. I told the guy I'd think about it, hung up, and sold the remainder of our shares as quickly as I could, thanking my lucky stars—and Giraffe's risk control measures—that got us out with a loss of a "mere" 33 percent.

Of course, I was being a fool twice over. The first time I was a fool for buying the stock of an indebted company that was doing a favor to its clients. This was foolishness number one, committed because I thought I knew so much about the company—far more than anyone else—that all others were wrong. The fact the CEO and his lieutenants were buying, of course, gave me extra comfort, but perhaps also made me a bit too relaxed about checking further.

I made up for some of that foolishness by getting out of the stock once it hit our maximum risk point. But once I sold, I immediately became a fool a second time for not going short!

I mean, I was just handed a piece of iron-clad information that much more of the common stock's value would be grabbed by the debenture holders. This meant the stock would plunge further. Yet I was so busy feeling relief at being out of the stock—and at not feeling foolish anymore—that I did not see this obvious opportunity.

So I not only lost money on a bad pick, I missed the opportunity to make the money back—plus more—by reversing my position. This was foolishness squared. I had been a fool once, okay. But at least I should've allowed the fool to make some money.

Let this then be a quintuple lesson to you.

First, even when you end up knowing mostly everything about a company through sleuthing, don't let it go to your head. Check the public information—what you don't know can trip you just the same, perhaps even more so, because you are already cocky with knowing some physical facts that few others do.

Second, be very careful about investing in companies with debt. Revenues, profits, costs, all can come and go, but debt is forever. Or, as newsletter writer Jim Grant used to put it, "Debt is always repaid, either by the borrower or by the lender." Therefore, if in doubt about a terrific bargain stock that also has some debt, stay out of it.

Third, be careful of companies at the very peak of a technology pyramid. In the worst case, they risk being made obsolete altogether; in the best case, they may need to keep running faster and faster just to stay in one place—in effect doing a favor to their customers.

Fourth, do not view insider buying as infallible. Yes, it's mostly a good indication. But insiders can be wrong, too. In the case of SCI, the charismatic CEO convinced himself that the future was bright and, because of his charisma, managed to convince those around him to buy also. All were wrong.

Fifth and last, be humble. Even when you sleuth a company diligently, you can still be wrong. Never put too much into any one stock—even if you think you are absolutely sure. *Especially* if you think you are absolutely sure. Never go for broke, because you may get there. The successful sleuth investor is the liquid sleuth investor. Irrational acts can and do happen—such as the massive buying by SCI's insiders or even their decision to stay in a no-growth business.

SUPERFIBERCO

The second blooper is a cautionary tale of another sort. It exemplifies the wisdom of the popular warning that even if you know a lot about someone, you still cannot be certain of what he or she might do.

SuperFiberCo was (and still is) a sizable company making a range of equipment for optical communications. I have always admired the company, defining it firmly as a "goody." It was not a fast-rising rocket, but neither was it a dead behemoth, and it was growing fast enough. However, it was never a "cheapy," or at least not cheap enough for Giraffe's stingy tastes, and so I never invested in the stock. One day, however, I read about a pending strike in SuperFiberCo's main plant, located near its headquarters in a midsize town in the Northeast. At this bit of news my ears perked up. I love strikes. They look like disasters but rarely are, except in huge union shop behemoths like the car companies. There they indicate deep-seated problems of mistrust which prevent the company from ever being a goody. But elsewhere, strikes are usually transitory issues, especially if they are only about issues of pay. If they knock the price of a goody, this could present an opportunity.

At SuperFiberCo the strike was merely about issues of pay. (Or so I thought.) A large Japanese company had awarded SuperFiberCo a major contract to make fiber optical cable capable of possible transmission of laser signals over hundreds of miles without the need for a "repeater" every few miles (as the old glass fiber required). Only two manufacturers in the world could make such a fiber—a competitor of the Japanese prospective client and SuperFiberCo. But because the Japanese customer was loath to give the order to its competitor, it decided to award it to SuperFiberCo. It was further understood that if SuperFiberCo could fulfill the order well, it had a good chance to get orders double and triple this size in the following years. How did I learn all this? From chatting with telecom engineers, because I needed the knowledge peripherally for some other investments. Yet because SuperFiberCo was never cheap enough, it was never a potential investment for me until the strike threat.

Because the union in the plant that made the fiber cable had not seen a raise for two years, it saw the new contract as an excellent opportunity to extract concessions from management, under the threat of a strike. Unless union members received certain wage raises and some benefits, they would walk off the job, they said. Management of SuperFiberCo offered less than the union desired, and so the two sides huffed and puffed before the deadline set by the union, while meeting daily in the local union hall for negotiating sessions. The matter dragged on.

This did not worry me much, however. Usually such negotiations are settled one hour (or minute) before the deadline, since no negotiator can return to his constituency with concessions unless he or she can prove he had no choice, other than everyone losing their jobs. Because I was fairly sure this would be the case here, and because the stock had already fallen a lot on the strike threat, I did some preliminary sleuthing over the phone and via some industry informants. The primary checks came up good. The strike was unlikely to happen, and both sides were being reasonably rational. The situation, in other words, deserved deeper due diligence without much risk of wasting my time. So I booked a flight to that midsize town in the Northeast where SuperFiberCo's plant was located, reserved a room in the local Holiday Inn, and flew in.

I spent the next few days chatting with union members in their union hall, with local reporters of the free weekly papers (who often know everything), and with a variety of managers of pool halls, bowling alleys, and other establishments who have their fingers on the pulse of their clientele, which were the blue-collar employees of SuperFiberCo. Finally, I also met with management. I had a pleasant lunch with the human resources negotiator, a kindly gentleman who fed me roast beef and mashed potatoes in the company's country club-cum-golf course-cum-corporate hangout. The impression I got was of two positions not so far apart. Furthermore, the day before I was to return to Toronto, the Japanese customer issued a polite threat, couched in bureaucratic jargon, but a threat just the same—saying, in effect, that if there were a strike, the contract would be yanked, as would some other orders they had already placed with the company. This, to everyone's shock, meant that not only would there be no raises, but that perhaps 100 out of 800 jobs might be lost.

Both the union and the company negotiators understood this. So did the union rank and file. It seemed to me a foregone conclusion that the new contract would be signed before the week was out.

I flew back to Toronto, where I bought a moderate amount of SuperFiberCo stock at about $9 a share, aiming to sell some of it at 50 percent higher once the strike was settled, intending to keep the rest for a long-term investment.

Human beings, I figured, don't shoot themselves in the foot.

But apparently they do, or, rather, the situation may not be what you read in the press or in analysts' reports. The strike vote I saw as a surefire "No" came out overwhelmingly in favor of a strike. The entire plant's rank and file walked out, and there were even a few acts of vandalism that messed up the production line to such an extent that it was clear that even if work resumed, it would be six months before high-quality fiber could be made there again.

Everyone was shocked. The *Wall Street Journal* wrote articles blaming union agitators, who were supposedly making a career on the back of fired employees. The local newspaper editorial dumped on the company. So did Wall Street. Investors dumped the stock. When it reached $7, I began to sell. At 6½ I was out—angry, bewildered, and perplexed.

What happened? How come all my sleuthing did not anticipate the coming strike? What had changed during the day between my departure and the strike vote?

I called some of my union contacts. Even those who had been friendly before were taciturn now. None wanted to say anything. Finally, at long last, I managed to extract the story from the one person who usually knows more than most, the reporter for the local free weekly. What happened was this:

The week before the strike vote, a senior machinist at the plant asked the shop steward to ask management if he could rent the company's golf club-cum-country club-cum-cafeteria (where I had eaten lunch with the HR guy) for his daughter's wedding. He had a large family and more were coming from Italy for the occasion, and the largest hall in town that could accommodate them was not nice enough, and the guy wanted to impress his Italian family, since some of his wife's relatives were of the hoity-toity sort. At any rate, the corporate country club facility had been rented out once before, to one of the VPs for some of his family functions. The machinist was willing to pay for the rental—the machinist wanted to give his only daughter a memorable wedding.

Well, the answer came back that, unfortunately, the place was already taken for that entire week for a corporate function, a training seminar or some such.

The machinist went ahead and rented a hall in town, the wedding went ahead, and although it was a success, he did get back snippy and sniffy comments from the Italy-resident wife's family.

I asked the reporter how all this was connected to the strike.

Well, he said, the machinist's nephew, a bright lad, was also working as a caddy for one of the company's VPs, and during one of the golf games, he heard the VP say that the hall was available that week, but that the club's committee had decided not to rent it out to the machinist because, "then we'd have to fumigate the washrooms for a month."

This comment went back to his uncle, who told his friends in the union hall. The strike issue was suddenly transformed from a question of money into a question of respect. Not only did management separate themselves physically from employees by having their own club, but they deemed employees too unclean to share the premises with them. What other means did the employees have of registering their anger but a strike?

Which is what they did. The strike lasted four months. The Japanese yanked their order. Perhaps 80 employees had to be let go, including two VPs. The caddy lost his job, too. Everyone seemed intent on shooting themselves in the foot. It was clear that it would be a year or more before the plant could recover.

The stock fell to $4. As in the case of SuperfastComputer Inc, I felt so relieved at having sold it that I did not see the additional gift I was handed: at $4 the stock was trading a snick below book value. And it was clear that the company, which had existed 80 years already, would probably be in existence at least 8 more. Or perhaps even 80? No matter. My relief at getting out with a minor loss blinded me, and I did not buy the stock again after selling it. It, of course, rose again, once the strike was settled. How far did it go? Would you believe me if I told you it went to $28? Yes. I had missed a seven-bagger because of wounded pride.

The conclusions I drew from this episode are the following:

1. Even commercial people do not always act in their own financial self-interest. Quite often other needs dominate and even swamp rational considerations.

2. No matter how much you learn about people, you can never predict their behavior.

3. Occasionally, what seems to others a minor matter may act as a trigger to a larger action that changes the course of events—especially in matters of contention.

4. When you mess up an investment, get out of the stock to clear your mind and emotions, but do not let the shame of having messed up prevent you from keeping the stock on your radar screen. As I noted in my previous blooper with SCI, if you have been foolish but 'fessed up, the pardoned fool can now at least make some money with his expensively acquired wisdom.

5. When a stock of a solid company with tradition, history, and good finances falls on hard times, so long as the balance sheet remains strong, the stock may be worth sleuthing once it becomes ridiculously cheap. But not before.

EPILOGUE:
CASE CLOSED

I explained in the Introduction that I wrote this book because there's enough foolish money for all of us to share. But there's another reason. After years of sleuthing, I realized that for many good people, work is a life-deadening experience. Because I made a lot of money talking to such people, I felt an obligation to help them. Finally, I concluded that the best way to do so was to show them how to become so rich they wouldn't have to work unless they wanted to. This book aspires to help you change your mindset from that of an agent, an employee, to that of a principal.

AGENTS AND PRINCIPALS

What is the difference? Agents are like hunting dogs, while principals are like wolves. The two may look similar, but the difference between them is profound. Hunting dogs need a master who will pay them a wage, tell them what to hunt, appropriate their catch, and throw them a bonus bone. The CEO of Morgan Stanley is an agent. Though highly compensated, he is really a peddler of other people's companies. He is paid a wage and a bonus, and he is given stock options. But he doesn't own the company; he works for the owners, which, in this case, are the public. He is paid to hunt.

A wolf, on the other hand, hunts only for itself and its family. It works for no one, hunts what it pleases, and the game it catches belongs to it alone, although it may share with other wolves that partnered in the hunt. The owner of the corner hamburger joint is a principal. His business may be small and he may earn less than the secretary of Morgan Stanley's chief, but he owns the place, and if it grows through franchising, he and his family can make a large profit.

But the difference between agents and principals is more than just ownership. The real, primal differences are who you take your orders from and for whose benefit you are working. Principals take orders from themselves and their customers, and work for their family's benefit. Agents take orders from the master, and work for the benefit of the master's family, not theirs. Even real sleuths are only agents, working for others, not for themselves.

The above should not be read as a disparagement of agents. Without them, companies would have no employees, and you and I would have no stocks to buy, nor brokers to buy and sell them for us. There is a role for everyone in life. However, my aim is not to teach you how to climb the corporate ladder to become Top Corporate Dog. There are many other books that do that, if that's your game. Rather, I want to show you how to become privately rich, so that you can have a choice regarding whether you'd like to work or not. And to get there, you must start thinking like a principal—people who work for themselves and their family, not for others.

Why do most agents work for others? To paraphrase that most American of aphorisms, they value comfort over freedom and so often end up with neither. On the other hand, principals value freedom over comfort, and so often get both. If you do some of what I describe, you will inevitably become richer, perhaps very rich. What I cannot tell you is whether you'll choose to keep working once you've made your fortune.

Will you? Many lottery winners do, you know. I personally know seven lottery winners (four policemen and three firemen in a small Ontario town) who won $43 million in the lottery, or a bit more than $6 million each. After taking a joint cruise and paying off their mortgages and buying a few cars, they went right back to work. I called them and asked why. (As you already know, I am not shy about calling strangers and asking them questions.)

Well, they all sheepishly admitted, they went back to work because they enjoyed what they did and it made them feel useful. Besides, a person must have a place to go when he or she wakes up in the morning, no? How long can you play golf?

In the same vein, I am told that some old-line CIA employees—real sleuths—were independently wealthy and worked for the "Agency" out of a sense of obligation, not out of need for a job (and perhaps because they, too, needed a place to go to in the morning, where they'd feel useful). They were their own masters, but still served their country—not their bosses' families or their bosses' careers. They could not be browbeaten or scared into changing their true views by threats of losing their livelihood or status, because they already had both. Thus, their work only benefited from their independence, as did the Agency, and the country.

Would you choose to continue working after you made your fortune? Or would you quit and write that novel or sail the Caribbean or buy that longhorn cattle farm? Or perhaps you, too, once you've learned how, would keep sleuthing, to take the fools' money for pleasure, even when you no longer need it, wouldn't you?

It's up to you. But first you should have the choice, and to have it you must have enough money to make work optional. This book should help you get it. So go ahead and use what you have learned. Good sleuthing and good luck!

GIVING BACK

Finally, let me address one of the greatest benefits of successful sleuthing and profitable investing: the opportunity to give back. Most people contribute to charity via an organization of their choice, which, in turn, chooses the recipients. This is a worthwhile use of money and is tax deductible too. But an even more satisfying activity is to sleuth for true needs on your own, using methods similar to those that made you your money; then give anonymously to a needy person of your choosing, via an intermediary. You would do this not instead of other charitable giving, but on top of it.

For example, how about fulfilling the wish of that bright young waitress who confided to you that her dream is to study fashion design? Since you are such a good listener now, not only did she tell you this, but also that she's taking care of her mother and cannot afford the full year of study. You make a mental note of it, and once back at your office, for the price of a small used car, you can have your lawyer send her a check that would make her dream come true, anonymously. Your only two modest requirements: that she confirm receipt of the money and that she write a letter at the end of the year describing how she had used it. Believe me, that letter would give you far more enjoyment than another car. If you really want to wring the last ounce of satisfaction out of it, you can also go sit at the back of her first fashion show, to see her first creation. But it'd be better to use that time to sleuth for more need elsewhere.

Another option would be dropping in to chat with some teenagers at the local shelter, to find out what their favorite food is, and then take them to a good restaurant that serves it, and chat with them further. They are starved for attention, the same as corporate employees are (probably more so). Yes, this would not be anonymous, but at a certain point you are allowed to indulge. Or, if you prefer to maintain anonymity, you can give the money to the shelter's manager, who'll take them to the restaurant and listen to them talk. (You can trust him or her to do so—there are few people on earth you can trust more.)

What about the tax deduction, you say? It is true that none of these activities is tax deductible. But so what? An organized charity spends some of your contribution on organization and on seeking out need—all necessary and worthwhile acts, to be sure—but this means that only part of your contribution reaches the final destination. You should keep giving to such organizations, of course, but if you also sleuth for need yourself, you can have the extra benefit of knowing exactly where it goes.

Lump such giving in the same category as buying another car or another boat—an indulgence. Try it. Once you do it once, there'll be more. Trust me on this.

Where to find such need? Oh, it is everywhere. Wherever and when-ever people let themselves be convinced they are mere agents for others, not for themselves and their families, you'll find the needy. So when you have learned to act like a principal and have become rich as a result, you have a certain obligation to help those less fortunate. Sprinkle gold dust wherever you go, anonymously, and more will come to you, somehow. The same skills and mindset (and heartset) are needed for both. In the final count, it is all of one piece.

WHERE TO DIG FOR PUBLIC INFORMATION

CORPORATE FILINGS

SEC's Edgar site: www.sec.gov/edgar

Barron's weekly compilation of significant buys and sells by insiders; Barron's weekly compilation of 13D transactions

Canada: www.sedar.com

INSIDER TRADING

United States: www.insidercow.com; finance.yahoo.com, insiders' transactions

Canada: www.sedi.ca

BACKGROUND ON COMPANIES

Directors' biographies: Reuters website

Stories behind companies: *Forbes, Fortune, BusinessWeek, Barron's, New York Observer* (yes), and other organs of the popular press

CHAT-UP TECHNIQUES
Neuro-Linguistic-Programming: The Structure of Magic, Richard Bandler and John Grinder
Patterns of Hypnotic Techniques of Milton Erickson, books I and II, Richard Bandler and John Grinder

SURVEILLANCE TECHNIQUES
Advanced Surveillance, Peter Jenkins

INSTINCTIVE DECISION MAKING
Blink, Malcolm Gladwell

SOURCES FOR VALUE INVESTORS
The Intelligent Investor, Benjamin Graham and David L. Dodd
Common Stocks and Uncommon Profits, Philip A. Fisher
Market Wizards series, Jack D. Schwager
Reminiscences of a Stock Operator, Edwin LeFevre
Web site telling you about great investors: www.streetstories.com/
Margin of Safety, Seth Klarman (Note: This book is out of print and most library copies have been stolen. But if you manage to find one copy, read it attentively.)
A Random Walk Down Wall Street, Burton Malkiel (A book commonly read by members of the opposition, whose money you aim to take.)
A reasonable summary of the efficient market theory (a.k.a. efficient market hypothesis) in all its forms (strong, semistrong, and weak): www.investopedia.com (Please note, not once is the word *physical* mentioned.)
Alan Turing's 1936 paper: "Can Machines Think?" in *The World of Mathematics*, Volume II, John Newman. The paper can also be found at www.abelard.org/turpap/turpap.htm (Nine contrary views on the main question are offered. None of the nine, by the way, includes the full sensory perception-physical argument.)

OTHER BOOKS OF INTEREST

Class: A Guide to the American Status System, Paul Fussell

Endogenous Economic Fluctuations, Mordecai Kurz

Goedel's Proof, Ernest Nagel, James R. Newman, edited by Douglas R.
  Hofstadter

IF YOU CAN DO STOCKS BY NUMBERS, WHY NOT NOVELS?

EMT AND ELT (EFFICIENT LITERARY THEORY): A COMPARISON

To convey the full silliness of treating the human drama of commerce exclusively by math, let's construct here, on the fly, a similar mathematical theory for novels, using the same mathematical jargon and word format that Nobel-winning economists use when they write about stocks. To do this, we'll view a best-selling stock as analogous to a best-selling novel, that is, a dramatic story with characters in action, encapsulated either in a piece of paper or a screen, which many people want and spend money to own.

Here then is the efficient literary theory.

Assume the universe of all n novels is $N(i)$ ($i = 1$ to n), where each novel i possesses m literary qualities $L(i, j)$, ($j = 1$ to m), so that each novel can be described exhaustively and completely (note the hidden assumptions here) by $F(L(i, j))$, when F is a single-valued and nonsingular function for all i and j, mapping from the domain N into the domain $B(k)$, (k = 1 to n), where $B(k)$ is the ordered list of all U.S. novels, sorted by their place on the best-seller list as measured by numbers of copies sold. (Alternatively, the number of copies sold can be divided by the U.S. population at the time, to adjust for population growth.)

As a side comment, please note that this would be equivalent to EMT's stocks and securities (Sharpe's, Markowitz's, or Malkiel's) being represented only by the random fluctuations of their prices, or a company's riskiness being represented only by the Mertonian squiggliness of its past stock prices (a.k.a. as volatility, or beta).

I could develop this theory further, even expand it to include multidimensional space, use vectors and tensors, and employ a variety of formulas to reach some nonobvious conclusions, and then publish scientific papers. (There are quite a number of such papers in EMT on the same level as the above theory. But I digress.)

Once we have such a theory, we can start checking it against reality—taking our cue from EMT—by using data. The data would, of course, have to be numerical, since our theory is mathematical. Characters and conflicts and drama and plot would have no place in the theory. Indeed the mathematical model would be blind to them, just as the limp handshake of a sales VP and the rolled eyes and alcoholic breath of a CEO's son would have no place in EMT, nor gut feeling that someone is lying. However, there's plenty of numbers for us to use in ELT—whether they are relevant for forecasting the novel's value (or at least its place on the best-seller list) is not in question, because when checking a mathematical theory, what else *can* we use but numbers? And so, for a large database of novels (say all novels sold over the last 50 years in the United States for which we have sales records), we can count the number of words, length of each word, length of paragraphs, length of chapters, number of chapters, frequency of all letters and of words, perhaps even the number of vowels and consonants, sibilants, fricatives, and plosives—indeed, any quantity that our mapping system (math) can capture after being converted to numbers. Why, we can even encode the color of the paper or (getting sophisticated here) the weight of a novel or even its physical size.

Then, just as EMT and its offspring index funds attempt to help investors to make money (or, rather, prevent them from losing money by showing them it's proven to be hopeless) via statistics of the price fluctuation, so we can now correlate each novel's sales with the mass of numerical data we have assembled, to find which of these could help us write a best-selling novel. Should we use long words or short? Pink paper or white? Many chapters or few? Do quarto-size books sell better than folio-size? Big fonts or small fonts? Big caps or small caps? How about long sentences versus short ones? Since we have lots of data, and next-to-free labor in the form of graduate students of ELT, we can try all manners of possible correlations between parts of our vast database and a novel's place on the best-seller list—just as mathematical finance mavens and quants try to forecast a stock's place on the best-selling stocks list, using their vast numerical databases.

Astonishingly, and as EMTers do in finance, our ELT mavens find that there is next to no correlation! None of these variables can forecast which novel will sell well, which poorly, and so we must conclude that one cannot write a best-selling novel without having "inside information" about what makes the managers at Barnes & Noble put one novel in the front of the store and another one in the back—or what makes the *New York Times* literary editors put one novel higher than another on the list. And if a writer's goal is to write a best-selling novel, the ELT database provides no help—just as the vast stock databases appear to be of little help to investors who want to pick best-selling stocks. The ELT numbers, in short, prove conclusively and depressingly that writing a best-selling novel is a random event, not skill, and therefore, estimating its literary value or sales prospects are all due to insiders' knowledge of bookstore management and literary supplements' editorial policies. One might as well put a chimpanzee to hit and peck at typewriter keys (perhaps one of those simians who had survived the stock picking contest?), rather than learn how to write novels. Math has just proved that it is hopeless.

Now, old-timers may quibble with ELT and say that some hidden qualities of books cannot be captured by math, such as characters of the dramatis personae, the quality of conflict, or the writing ability—just as EMT cannot capture the character of managements, the quality of the business, or management's execution ability. But, just as does EMT for stocks, so will ELT assume for novels that anything not expressible in math is of negligible importance—at any rate small enough to be neglected.

Using the above assumption, an entirely new academic field of literary theory can be constructed and inserted holus-bolus into departments of literary criticism, to be called, say, modern literary theory, or efficient literary theory. It would have vast implications for the future literary market—just as EMT had for the financial markets. It will also have a salubrious effect on math education, since all English PhDs will now be required to take Math 101-401 (just as budding investors now must) and write learned papers using mathematical symbols only.

Or perhaps the new field has already been incorporated into literary theory, judging by the latest *New York Times* best-seller list. I would politely suspend judgment, but I must point to two French literary theorists, Messrs. Jacques Derrida and Jacques Lacan, who have arguably done just that and launched the field of ELT very creditably. And, who knows? Perhaps in the future, a Nobel Prize for Literature will be awarded to some ELT professor, forecasting a novel's sales by its weight, word stats, and other mathematical fauna. After all, if the Nobel Prize for Economics has been awarded to statisticians of price fluctuations, why not the same for literature theory scientists? Advances in human knowledge can come from many a corner—but so, unhappily, have regressions in knowledge, masquerading as advances.

A vner Mandelman is founder and CEO of Giraffe Capital Corporation, one of Canada's most successful private investment firms. A recognized investing expert and television stock commentator, Mandelman spends much of his time sleuthing companies throughout North America. He writes a biweekly column for the *Globe & Mail* and his articles have appeared in *Barron's*. Mandelman is also the author of the prize-winning story collection, *Talking to the Enemy*.